DO-IT-YOURSELF GUIDES

Step-By-Step Kitchen & Bath Projects

Quality tools to build your world.

ACKNOWLEDGEMENTS

Created by Creative Publishing international
in conjunction with WSP Marketing International Ltd.,
47 Valleybrook Drive, Don Mills, Ontario M3B 2S6,
Canada.

**Creative Publishing international
Book Development Staff**

Vikki Anderson
Shawn Binkowski
Steve Boman
Janice Cauley
Marcia Chambers
Maren Christensen
Paul Currie
Doug Deutscher
Melissa Erickson
Jacque Fletcher
John Fletcher
Brad Kissell
Janet Lawrence
Bill Nelson
Chuck Nields
Jon Simpson
Greg Wallace
Gina Wornson

Printed on Canadian paper by World Color
Book Services, USA.

ISBN 0-86573-762-2

This book provides useful instructions but
we cannot anticipate all of your working
conditions or the characteristics of your
materials and tools. For safety, you should
use caution, care and good judgement
when following the procedures described
in this book. Consider your own skill level
and the instructions and safety precautions
associated with the various tools and
materials shown.

Creative Publishing international, WSP
Marketing International Ltd., Canadian Tire
Corporation, Ltd. or the Canadian Tire
Associate Dealers do not assume any
responsibility for damage to property
or injury to persons as a result of the use
of the information contained in this book.

Before commencing any project, consult
your local Building Department for information on building permits, codes and
other laws, as they may apply to
your project.

INTRODUCTION

Of the many rooms in your home, kitchens and baths suffer the most wear-and-tear, and they often have to be adapted to your family's changing needs. While major renovations often require the use of professionals, with the right information you can do many of the smaller remodelling projects in these rooms yourself. *Step-By-Step Kitchen & Bath Projects* will give you the confidence you need to do this work, and will save you both time and money. You'll see which Mastercraft tools you need and the proper techniques for using them, as well as information about the best materials to choose for your remodelling projects.

Step-By-Step Kitchen & Bath Projects is divided into sections which cover major kitchen and bathroom elements. Each section contains the kind of information you need to know before beginning remodelling projects, including how to work safely and any work area preparations you may need to make. Then, individual projects are demonstrated with detailed, step-by-step instructions and full-colour photographs. You'll also see the specific tools and materials each project requires. Throughout each section you will find tips about tools, materials and project techniques that will make your work as simple and efficient as possible.

Now you can make your kitchen and bath more functional and enjoyable – and save time and money, too. Welcome to the world of Mastercraft Do-It-Yourself Guides!

TABLE OF CONTENTS

TOOLS

To successfully make the remodelling projects seen in this book you need the proper tools, and they are shown here. Quality tools, like Mastercraft, will serve your needs well. Keep hand tools protected and organized by storing them in a tool-box. This also will allow you to easily carry them to the project site. Shelves or cabinets are good locations for power tools and other specialty tools and supplies.

Basic hand tools: *caulk gun (A), putty knife (B), pry bar/nail puller (C), work gloves (D), ear protection (E), carpenter's square (F), level (G), work light (H), chisels (I), sponge (J), eye protection (K), pencil (L), felt-tipped pen (M), mallet (N), hammer (O), awl (P), file (Q), nail set (R), dust mask (S), chalk line (T), hex key wrenches (U), utility knife (V), sand paper (W), needlenose pliers (X), Robo-Grip® pliers (Y), groove joint pliers (Z), screwdrivers (AA), clamps – C & bar (BB), hacksaw (CC), tape measure (DD), scissors (EE), handsaw (FF), stud finder (GG), straightedge (HH).*

Power tools: *circular saw (A), palm sander (B), belt sander (C), jigsaw (D), drill (E), drill bits, including screwdriver bits (F), reciprocating saw (G).*

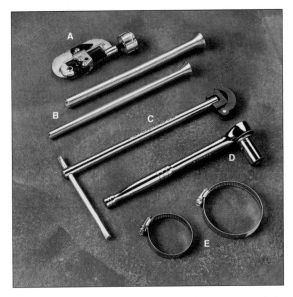

Specialty plumbing tools: *tubing cutter (A), tubing benders (B), basin wrench (C), ratchet wrench with socket (D), hose clamps (E).*

Flooring tools: *hand maul (A), end cutters (B), 100-lb. floor roller (C), linoleum roller (D), floor scraper (E), staple gun (F), nail puller (G).*

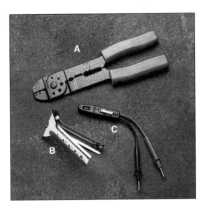

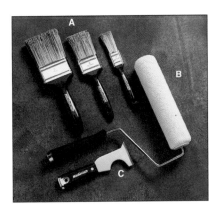

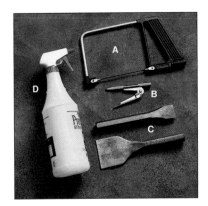

Specialty electrical tools: *wire stripper (A), cable stripper (B) neon circuit tester (C).*

Painting tools: *brushes (A), roller (B), scraper (C).*

Other tools: *rod saw (A), compass (B), masonry chisels (C), spray bottle (D).*

Principles of Kitchen Design

As you begin to plan your new kitchen, keep in mind the principles of kitchen design. Use these principles to help evaluate the efficiency of your new kitchen.

Create a floor plan. Experiment with different arrangements. A kitchen design kit available at bookstores and home improvement centres helps create new designs.

Seek professional advice. Discuss your final plans with a Certified Kitchen Designer (CKD) or an architect.

Establish work areas. A kitchen has three major work areas for (illustration right): 1) food preparation, including the refrigerator and food storage cabinets; 2) cooking, built around the range/oven and the microwave; and 3) clean-up, combining the sink, dishwasher and garbage disposer.

Establish the kitchen work triangle. A triangular arrangement of work areas is the classic of kitchen design (illustration above right). It helps make efficient use of food preparation, cooking and clean-up areas. To create the kitchen triangle, add the distances between the major work areas. The total should be no less than 12' and no more than 21'. A smaller triangle means the work spaces are too crowded. A larger triangle indicates that steps are wasted.

Plan adequate counter space. The recommended minimums are: 24" on each side of cooking appliances, 24" on

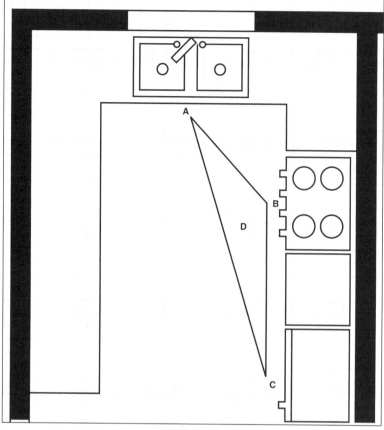

Layout for kitchen: sink (A), stove (B), refrigerator (C), work triangle (D).

each side of the sink area and 18" next to a refrigerator.

Store items for easy access. Cabinets near any one work area should contain related items.

Establish a work schedule. The time it takes to alter a kitchen, no matter how brief, is a disruption. If you hire professionals for portions of the job, be sure to get estimates for time as well as materials and labour. Obtain all necessary building permits for the portions of the work you will do yourself. Make sure your project meets all local Building Codes (see pages 10-11).

Principles of Bathroom Design

After you have reached a decision about the type of bathroom you want, make a specific and thorough bathroom plan.

You will need to make drawings and a materials list, set budgets and time-tables, decide when to do the work yourself and when to hire help. You may also need to obtain a building permit and make arrangements to have your work inspected. Remember, a bathroom update can be as simple as replacing an out-of-date or unattractive sink faucet.

To simplify your remodelling project, use existing plumbing and wiring wherever possible. If you plan to remove part or all of a wall to expand your bathroom, determine whether the wall is load-bearing before you cut any wall studs. If you are unsure about the special support requirements of load-bearing walls, contact your building inspector. Make sure your entire project conforms with all of your local Building Codes (see pages 10-11).

TIP:

If you have only one bathroom in your home, arrange for alternate accommodations while your remodelling project is under way.

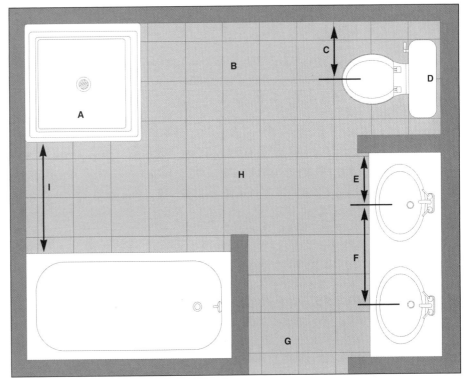

Follow minimum clearance and size guidelines to plan a comfortable, safe and easy-to-use bathroom. Shower base (A) 32" x 32", 30" x 30" minimum open space in front of toilet (B), 15" from centre of toilet (C) to wall or fixture, 1" between toilet tank (D) and wall, 12" sink centre to wall (E), 30" between sink centres (F), 32" of clear walkway at entrance (G), 21" of clear walkway in front of sink, toilet and bathing fixtures (H), 18" between bathtub and other fixtures (I).

Bathroom Planning & Design Checklist

❑ Include a vent fan (see page 60), even if your bathroom has natural ventilation.
❑ Install adequate lighting (see page 58).
❑ Install a ground-fault circuit-interrupter (GFCI) on all receptacles (see page 59), and wire all bathroom circuits through the GFCI.
❑ Do not install a light switch within 60" of any bathtub or shower.
❑ All light fixtures above showers and tubs must be vapourproof (see page 58).
❑ Maintain a distance of at least 6" between major bathroom fixtures (some fixtures will need more, such as the 18" required by a bathtub).
❑ Bathtub faucets should be accessible from outside of the tub.
❑ Install at least one grab bar at the entrance to a tub or shower.
❑ Shower door must swing out, away from the shower.
❑ Use non-slip flooring material (see pages 12-25).
❑ Add an anti-scald device to showers to protect against burns.

Learn about Codes

To ensure public safety, your community requires that you get a permit to install new wiring and have the completed work reviewed by an appointed inspector. Electrical inspectors use the Canadian Electrical Code (C.E.C.) as the primary authority for evaluating wiring, but they also follow the local Building Code and Electrical Code standards.

As you begin planning new circuits, call or visit your local electrical inspector to discuss the project. The inspector can tell you which of the national and local Code requirements apply to your job, and may give you a packet of information summarizing these regulations. Later, when you apply for a work permit, the inspector will expect you to understand the local guidelines as well as a few basic C.E.C. requirements.

The Canadian Electrical Code is a set of standards that provides minimum safety requirements for wiring installations. It is revised every three years. The C.E.C. requirements for the projects shown in this book are thoroughly explained on the following pages. For more information, you can find copies of the current C.E.C., as well as a number of excellent handbooks based on the C.E.C., at libraries and bookstores.

In addition to being the final authority on Code requirements, inspectors are electrical professionals with years of experience. Although they have busy schedules, most inspectors are happy to answer questions and help you design well-planned circuits.

Basic Electrical Code Requirements:

Living areas need at least one 15-amp or 20-amp basic lighting/receptacle circuit for each 600 sq. ft. of living space, and should have a "dedicated" circuit for each type of permanent appliance. Receptacles on basic lighting/receptacle circuits should be spaced no more than 12' apart. Any wall more than 24" wide also needs a receptacle. Every room should have a wall switch that controls either a ceiling light or plug-in lamp.

❑ Stairways with six steps or more must have lighting that illuminates each step. The light fixture must be controlled by three-way switches at the top and bottom landings.

❑ Receptacles near a water source, such as a sink, must be protected by a ground-fault circuit-interrupter (GFCI).

❑ Cables must be protected against damage by nails and screws by at least 1¼" of wood. When cables pass through 2x2 furring strips, protect the cables with metal nail guards.

❑ Larger closets and storage spaces need at least one light fixture that is controlled by a wall switch near the entrance. Prevent fire hazards by positioning the light fixtures so the outer globes are at least 12" away from all shelf areas.

❑ Hallways more than 10' long need at least one receptacle. All hallways should have a switch-controlled light fixture.

❑ A metal brace attached to framing members is required for ceiling fans and large light fixtures that are too heavy to be supported by an electrical box.

Understanding Plumbing Codes

The National Plumbing Code of Canada (N.P.C.C.) is the set of regulations that building officials and inspectors use to evaluate your project plans and the quality of your work. Codes vary from region to region, but most are based on the National Plumbing Code of Canada, the authority used in the development of this book.

Code books are available for reference at bookstores and government offices. However, they are highly technical, difficult-to-read manuals. More user-friendly for do-it-yourselfers are the variety of Code handbooks available at bookstores and libraries. These handbooks are based on the N.P.C.C., but are easier to read and include many helpful diagrams and photos. Remember that your local Plumbing Code always supersedes the National Code.

Getting a Permit

To ensure public safety, your community requires that you obtain a permit for most plumbing projects, including all the projects demonstrated in this book.

When you visit your city Building Inspection office to apply for a permit, the building official will want to review three drawings of your plumbing project: a site plan, a water supply diagram and a drain-waste-vent (DWV) diagram. These drawings are described on this page. If the official is satisfied that your project meets Code requirements, he or she will issue you a plumbing permit, which is your legal permission to begin work. The building official will also specify an inspection schedule for your project. As your project nears completion, you will be asked to arrange for an inspector to visit your home while the pipes are exposed and review the installation to ensure its safety.

The site plan shows the location of the water main and sewer main with respect to your yard and home. The distances from your foundation to the water main and from the foundation to the main sewer should be indicated on the site plan.

The water supply diagram shows the length of the hot and cold water pipes and the relation of the fixtures to one another. The inspector will use this diagram to determine the proper size for the new water supply pipes in your system.

A DWV diagram shows the routing of drain and vent pipes in your system. Make sure to indicate the lengths of drain pipes and the distances between fixtures. The inspector will use this diagram to determine if you have properly sized the drain traps, drain pipes and vent pipes in your project.

TIPS:

Amp ratings of receptacles must match the size of the circuit. A common mistake is to use 20-amp receptacles on 15-amp circuits – a potential cause of dangerous circuit overloads.

❖❖❖❖❖❖❖❖❖❖❖❖

Label new circuits on an index attached to the circuit breaker panel. List the rooms and appliances controlled by each circuit.

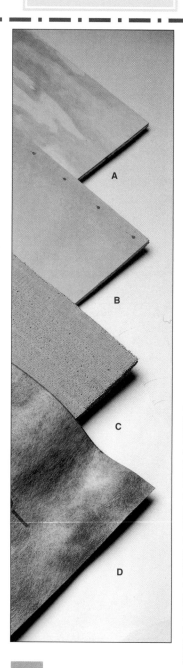

Project Preparation

Project preparation can range from simple to complex, depending on the condition of your existing floor. Providing a sound, smooth underlayment for your new flooring is a vital preparation step. This may involve only minor modifications to your existing floor, like applying embossing leveller. Or, the preparation required may involve complete underlayment removal and spot repairs to your subfloor. Avoid taking shortcuts, because they usually result in an inferior floor. If you are installing new underlayment, it is essential that you choose the right material. Before you get started, remove appliances or bathroom fixtures and prepare the room for more efficient and comfortable working conditions.

Selecting Underlayment Materials

Which type of underlayment (photo left) you should choose depends in part on the type of floor covering you will be installing. For example, ceramic and natural-stone floors require a rigid and stable underlayment that resists movement. Though you may use plywood or fibreboard under ceramic tile installations, cementboard is highly recommended. For resilient flooring, use a quality-grade plywood, since most manufacturers will void their warranty if their flooring is installed over substandard underlayment. Solid wood strip flooring and carpet do not require underlayment and are often placed directly on a plywood subfloor.

Plywood (A) is the most common underlayment for resilient flooring and ceramic tile installations. For resilient flooring, use ¼" exterior-grade AC plywood (at least one side perfectly smooth). Wood-based floor coverings, like parquet, can be installed over lower-quality exterior-grade plywood. For ceramic tile, use ½" AC plywood. Most manufacturers now recommend plywood over other wood-based, sheet-good underlayments.

Fibre/cementboard (B) is a thin, high-density underlayment used under ceramic tile and resilient flooring in situations where floor height is a concern. (For installation, follow steps for cementboard installation, see page 17.)

Cementboard (C) is used only for ceramic tile installations. It is completely stable, even when wet, and is therefore the best underlayment to use in areas likely to get wet, such as bathrooms. Cementboard is considerably more expensive than plywood.

Isolation membrane (D) is used to protect ceramic tile installations from movement that may occur on cracked concrete floors. It is used primarily for covering individual cracks with strips of membrane, but it can also be used over an entire floor. A specialty product, it is available from commercial tile distributors.

General Preparations

Undercut door casings with a hand saw to make room for thicker floor products. For vinyl and wood, use a scrap of underlayment and a piece of new flooring as a spacing guide. For ceramic tile, also take into account the height of the adhesive.

Ventilate the project room, especially when applying adhesives or removing old flooring. A box fan placed in an open window and directed outside creates good air movement.

Shovel old flooring debris from your house through a window and into a wheelbarrow to speed up removal work. Protect fragile plants near the window with sheets of plywood.

Cover doorways with sheet plastic to contain debris and dust during removal.

Cover air and heat vents with sheet plastic and masking tape to prevent dust from entering ductwork.

Remove base mouldings before preparing for ceramic, resilient and hardwood flooring installation. Carefully pry the mouldings from the wall with a Mastercraft flat pry bar, using a wallboard knife to protect wall surfaces. Number each piece to simplify reinstallation.

Latex patching compounds can be used to fill cracks and chips in old underlayment as well as to cover screw or nail heads and seams in new underlayment. Some products include separate dry and wet ingredients that need to be mixed before application; others are pre-mixed.

RECOMMENDED HAND TOOLS

BASIC HAND TOOLS

- masonry chisel
- flat pry bar
- crowbar
- long-handled floor scraper
- utility knife
- hand maul
- wallboard knife
- cat's paw
- specialty tools, such as the floor scraper, are available at rental centres (see Tool Library pages 6-7)

NEEDED MATERIALS

- plywood
- sheet plastic
- crowbar
- masking tape

Removing Floor Coverings

When old floor coverings must be removed – as is the case with most projects – thorough and careful removal work is essential to the quality of the new flooring installation. The difficulty of flooring removal depends on the type of floor covering and the method that was used to install it.

How to Remove Sheet Vinyl

1 Use a utility knife to cut old flooring into strips about 1' wide.

2 Pull up as much flooring as possible by hand.

3 Cut stubborn sheet vinyl into strips about 5" wide. Starting at a wall, peel up as much of the floor covering as possible. If felt backing remains, spray a solution of water and liquid dishwashing detergent under the surface layer to help separate felt backing.

4 Scrape up remaining sheet vinyl and backing, using a floor scraper. If necessary, spray the backing again with soap solution to loosen it. Sweep up debris, then finish the clean-up with a wet/dry vacuum.

How to Remove Vinyl Tiles

1 Starting at a loose seam, use a long-handled floor scraper to remove tiles. To remove stubborn tiles, soften the adhesive with a heat gun, then use a wallboard knife to pry up the tile and scrape off the underlying adhesive.

2 Remove stubborn adhesive or backing by wetting the floor with a soap solution, then scraping with a floor scraper.

How to Remove Ceramic Tile

1 Knock out tile using a hand maul and masonry chisel. If possible, start in a space between tiles where grout has loosened. Be careful when working around fragile fixtures, like drain flanges.

2 If you plan to reuse the underlayment, use a floor scraper to remove any remaining adhesive.

How to Remove Carpet

1 Using a utility knife, cut around metal threshold strips to free carpet. Remove threshold strips with a flat pry bar.

2 Cut carpet into small pieces. Roll up carpet and remove it from the room, then remove the padding. Padding is usually stapled to the floor and will typically come up in pieces as you roll it up.

3 Using end-cutting nippers or pliers, remove all staples from floor. If you plan to lay new carpet, do not remove tackless strips unless they are damaged. **OPTION:** To remove glued-down carpet, first cut it into strips with a utility knife, then pull up as much as you can. Scrape up remaining cushion material and adhesive with a floor scraper.

Removing Underlayment

It is often easiest (because of adhesives and damage) to remove the underlayment along with the old floor covering. Make sure to cut the flooring into manageable pieces. **WARNING:** Flooring removal releases flooring particles into the air. Flooring in homes built before 1960 often contained asbestos. Check with your local building inspector to see how to find out if the flooring in your home contains asbestos and what to do with it if it does.

How to Remove Underlayment

1 Adjust the cutting depth of the circular saw to equal the combined thickness of your floor covering and underlayment. Using a carbide-tipped blade, cut the floor covering and underlayment into pieces measuring about 3 sq. ft. (photo below).

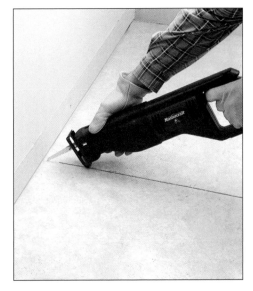

2 Use the reciprocating saw to extend cuts close to the edges of walls (photo above). Hold the blade at a slight angle to the floor, and try not to damage walls or cabinets. Use a wood chisel to complete cuts near cabinets.

3 Separate underlayment from subfloor, using a flat pry bar and hammer. Remove and discard the sections of underlayment and floor covering immediately.

Repairing Subfloors

After removing old underlayment, inspect the subfloor for loose seams, moisture damage, cracks and other flaws. If your subfloor is made of dimensional lumber rather than plywood, you can use plywood to patch damaged sections; if the plywood patch does not quite match the height of the subfloor, use floor leveller to raise its surface to the correct height.

RECOMMENDED POWER TOOLS

MASTERCRAFT

CIRCULAR SAW

MASTERCRAFT

RECIPROCATING SAW

RECOMMENDED HAND TOOLS

- basic hand tools
- eye protection
- wood chisel
- hand maul
- masonry chisel
- flat pry bar

TIPS:

You may have to use a belt sander with a coarse sanding belt to grind off stubborn adhesive.

❖❖❖❖❖❖❖❖❖❖

If your existing floor is ceramic tile over plywood underlayment, use a hand maul and masonry chisel to chip away tile along cutting lines before making cuts.

MASTERCRAFT

DRILL

MASTERCRAFT

CIRCULAR SAW

MASTERCRAFT

PALM SANDER

MASTERCRAFT

JIGSAW

RECOMMENDED HAND TOOLS

- basic hand tools
- wallboard knife
- countersink drill bit
- 1/8" & 1/4" notched trowels
- linoleum roller

NEEDED MATERIALS

- underlayment
- deck screws
- latex patching compound
- dry-set mortar
- fibreglass mesh tape

How to Apply Floor Leveller

1 Fill dips, chips or cracks in the subfloor with floor leveller. Mix leveller according to manufacturer's directions, then spread it on the subfloor with a trowel.

2 Check with a straightedge to make sure the filled area is even with the surrounding area; if not, apply more leveller. Allow leveller to dry, then shave off any ridges with the edge of a trowel, or sand smooth, if necessary.

How to Replace a Section of Subfloor

1 Mark a rectangle around the damaged area, with two sides centred over floor joists. Cut, using a circular saw with the blade adjusted to cut only through the subfloor. Use a chisel to cut near walls.

2 Remove damaged section, then nail two 2x4 blocks between joists, centred under the cut edges for added support. If possible, end nail blocks from below; otherwise toenail them from above.

3 Measure the cut-out section, then cut to fit, using material the same thickness as the original subfloor. Fasten to joists and blocks, using 2" deck screws spaced about 5" apart.

Installing Underlayment

When installing underlayment, make sure it is securely attached to the subfloor in all areas, including below all movable appliances.

How to Install Plywood Underlayment

1 Begin installing full sheets of plywood along the longest wall, making sure underlayment seams are not aligned with subfloor seams. Fasten plywood to the subfloor, using 1" screws driven every 6" along the edges and at 8" intervals throughout the rest of the sheet.

2 Continue fastening plywood to the subfloor, driving screw heads slightly below the underlayment surface. Leave 1/4" expansion gaps at the walls and between sheets. Offset seams in subsequent rows.

3 Using a circular saw or jigsaw, notch underlayment sheets to meet existing flooring in doorways, then fasten notched sheets to the subfloor.

4 Mix floor patching compound and latex or acrylic additive, according to the manufacturer's directions. Then, spread it over seams and screw heads with a wallboard knife.

5 Let patching compound dry, then sand patched areas smooth, using a power finishing sander.

TIP:
Notching the underlayment to properly fit room contours is often the most challenging task. A Mastercraft circular saw, jigsaw or handsaw can be used to accomplish this difficult step. Take time to measure carefully and transfer the correct measurements onto your underlayment. Rather than notching around door casings, you can undercut the casings and insert the underlayment beneath them.

How to Install Cementboard or Fibre/Cementboard Underlayment

1 Mix thin-set mortar according to manufacturer's recommendations. Starting at the longest wall, spread mortar on subfloor in a figure-eight pattern with a ¼" notched trowel (photo above). Spread mortar for one sheet at a time. Set the cementboard sheet on the mortar, smooth face up, making sure the edges are offset from subfloor seams.

2 Fasten cementboard to subfloor, using 1½" deck screws driven every 6" along edges and 8" throughout the sheet; drive screw heads flush with surface.

3 Cut cementboard pieces to fit, leaving a slight gap at the joints. For straight cuts, score a line with a utility knife, then snap the board along the score.

4 To cut holes, notches or irregular shapes, use a jigsaw with a carbide blade. Continue installing cementboard.

5 Place fibreglass mesh tape over seams, and spread a thin layer of thin-set mortar over the tape with a wallboard knife, feathering the edges. Cure mortar for two days.

How to Install Isolation Membrane

1 Thoroughly clean the subfloor, then apply thin-set mortar with a ⅛" notched trowel. Start spreading the mortar along a wall in a section as wide as the membrane, and 8' to 10' long. Check manufacturer's directions for mixing mortar.

2 Roll out the membrane over the mortar. Cut the membrane to fit tightly against the walls, using a straightedge and utility knife.

3 Starting in the centre of the membrane, use a linoleum roller to smooth out the surface toward the edges.

4 Repeat steps 1 through 3, cutting membrane as necessary at the walls. Do not overlap seams. Cure mortar for two days.

Installing Flooring in the Bathroom

Sheet vinyl (see page 18) and ceramic tile (see page 22) are the best bathroom flooring materials. Do not use highly porous underlayments, like lauan plywood, in bathrooms. Ceramic tile, when set into a bed of dry-set mortar over cementboard underlayment, is attractive and highly durable. Resilient vinyl floor tiles should be avoided in bathroom remodelling projects, because water can easily seep into the seams between tiles. Carpeting and hardwood are acceptable for dry areas, but are not recommended for wet areas in bathrooms.

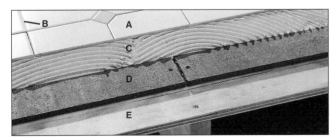

Anatomy of a ceramic tile floor: Unglazed ceramic floor tiles (A) finished with grout (B) are set into a bed of dry-set mortar (C). The mortar is applied over an underlayment of 5/8" cementboard (D) which is attached to the subfloor (E). The entire ceramic floor is covered with alkaline sealer.

Anatomy of a sheet-vinyl floor: Sheet-vinyl flooring (A) is bonded with vinyl flooring adhesive (B) to a new underlayment of ¼"-thick, exterior-grade plywood (C). The underlayment is nailed to the subfloor (D), which can be made from plywood or diagonal floorboards.

INSTALLING FLOORING

RECOMMENDED HAND TOOLS

MASTERCRAFT

BASIC HAND TOOLS

- staple gun
- linoleum or utility knife
- compass
- wallboard knife
- J-roller
- 100-lb. floor roller (for full-spread)

NEEDED MATERIALS

- template paper
- masking tape
- duct tape
- flooring adhesive
- metal threshold
- ⅜" staples

TIP:

Making a cutting template is the best way to ensure that your cuts will be correct. Use a Mastercraft tape measure, utility knife, some butcher paper and a felt-tipped pen to measure and mark contours accurately.

Installing Resilient Sheet Vinyl

After creating a near-perfect underlayment surface, for a successful installment cut the material so it fits perfectly along the contours of the room. When handling sheet vinyl, remember that this product – especially felt-backed – can crease and tear easily if mishandled. Many manufacturers require that you use their glue to install their flooring and will void their warranties if you do not follow their directions exactly.

How to Make a Cutting Template

1 Place sheets of heavy butcher's or postal-wrap paper along the walls, leaving a ¼" gap. Cut triangular holes in the paper with a utility knife (photo below). Fasten the template to the floor by placing masking tape over the holes.

2 Follow the outline of the room, working with one sheet of paper at a time. Overlap the edges of adjoining sheets by about 2", and tape the sheets together.

3 To fit the template around pipes, tape sheets of paper on either side. Measure the distance from the wall to the centre of the pipe, and subtract ⅛".

4 Transfer the measurement to a separate piece of paper. Use a compass to draw the pipe diameter onto the paper, then cut out the hole. Cut a slit from the edge of the paper to the hole.

5 Fit the hole cut-out around the pipe. Tape the hole template to adjoining sheets.

6 Roll or loosely fold the paper template for carrying.

How to Install Perimeter-bond Sheet Vinyl

1 Unroll the flooring on any large, flat, clean surface. To prevent wrinkles, sheet vinyl comes from the manufacturer rolled with the pattern side out. Unroll the sheet and turn it pattern side up for marking.

2 For two-piece installations, overlap the edges of sheets by at least 2". Plan seams to fall along the pattern lines or simulated grout joints. Align the sheets so that the pattern matches, then tape the sheets together with duct tape.

10 Lay seam edges, one at a time, into the adhesive. Make sure the seam is tight, pressing gaps together with your fingers. Roll the seam edges with a J-roller or wallpaper seam roller (photo left).

11 Apply flooring adhesive beneath flooring cuts at pipes or posts and around the entire perimeter of the room. Roll the flooring with the roller.

12 If applying flooring over a wood underlayment, fasten the outer edges of the sheet to the floor with ⅜" staples driven every 3" (photo below). Make sure the staples will be covered by the wall base moulding.

How to Install Full-spread Sheet Vinyl

1 Cut the sheet vinyl. (See pages 18-19, steps 1 to 5.) Then lay the sheet vinyl into position, sliding the edges underneath door casings.

2 Pull back half of the flooring, then apply a layer of flooring adhesive over the underlayment or old flooring, using a ¼" notched trowel. Lay flooring onto adhesive.

3 Roll the floor with a floor roller. Fold over the unbonded section of flooring. Wipe up any adhesive that oozes up around the edges of the vinyl with a damp rag.

4 Measure and cut metal threshold bars to fit across doorways, then position each bar over the edge of the vinyl flooring, and nail it in place.

3 Position the paper template over the sheet vinyl, and tape it into place. Trace the outline of the template onto the flooring with a non-permanent, felt-tipped pen.

4 Remove the template. Cut the sheet vinyl with a utility knife with a new sharp blade or a linoleum knife.

5 Cut holes for pipes and other permanent obstructions. Then cut a slit from the hole to the nearest edge of the flooring. Make slits along pattern lines, if possible.

6 Roll up flooring loosely and transfer it to the installation area. Do not fold flooring. Unroll and position the sheet vinyl carefully. Slide the edges beneath undercut door casings (see page 13).

7 Cut seams for two-piece installations, using a straightedge as a guide. Hold the straightedge tightly against the flooring, and cut along the pattern lines through both pieces of vinyl flooring.

8 Remove both pieces of scrap flooring. The pattern should now run continuously across the adjoining sheets of floor.

9 Fold back the edges of both sheets and apply a 3" band of multipurpose flooring adhesive to the underlayment or old flooring, using a wallboard knife or ¼" notched trowel.

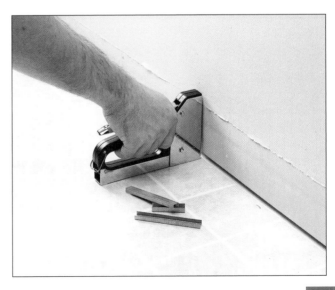

Installing Resilient Tile

Once the layout lines are established, the actual installation of the tile is relatively easy, especially if you are using self-adhesive tile. Make sure to check for noticeable directional features, like the grain of the vinyl particles. You can choose to set the tile in a running pattern, so the directional feature runs in the same direction, or you can set the tiles in a checkerboard pattern, called the quarter-turn method.

How to Establish Perpendicular Reference Lines for a Tile Installation

1 Position a reference line (X) by measuring opposite sides of the room and marking the centre of each side. Snap a chalk line between these marks.

2 Measure and mark the centrepoint of the chalk line. From this point, use a framing square to establish a second line perpendicular to the first. Snap a second reference line (Y) across the room (photo top right).

3 Check for squareness using the "3-4-5 triangle" method. Measure and mark one reference line 3' from the centrepoint on line (X). Measure and mark the other reference line 4' from the centrepoint on line (Y). Measure the distance between the marks (photo bottom right). If reference lines are perpendicular, the distance will measure exactly 5'. If not, adjust the reference lines until they are exactly perpendicular to one another.

How to Establish Tile Layout Lines

1 Snap perpendicular reference lines (X,Y) with a chalk line. Dry-fit tiles along one perpendicular layout line (Y). If necessary, you can shift the layout one way or the other to make the layout visually symmetrical or to reduce the number of tiles that need to be cut.

2 If you have shifted the tile layout, create a new line that is parallel to reference line (X) and runs through a tile joint near the original line. This new line (X1) will be one of the layout lines used when

RECOMMENDED HAND TOOLS

BASIC HAND TOOLS

- 1/16" notched trowel (for dry-back tile)
- chalk line
- framing square
- straightedge

NEEDED MATERIALS

- resilient tile
- flooring adhesive (for dry-back tile)
- metal threshold bars

installing the tile. Use a different-coloured chalk to distinguish between (X) and (X1).

3 Dry-fit tiles along the new layout line (X1). If necessary, adjust the layout, as in steps 1 and 2.

4 If you have adjusted the layout along line (X1), measure and mark a new layout line (Y1) that is parallel to the reference line (Y) and runs through one of the tile joints. This new line will form the second layout line you will use during installation.

How to Install Self-adhesive Resilient Tiles

1 Draw reference and layout lines (see instructions opposite page), make sure the surface is clean, then peel off the paper backing and install the first tile in one of the corners formed by the intersecting layout lines. Lay three or more tiles along each layout line in the quadrant. Rub the entire surface of each tile to bond the adhesive to the floor underlayment.

2 Begin installing tiles in the interior area of the quadrant (photo right). Make sure to keep joints between tiles tight.

3 Finish setting full-size tiles in the first quadrant, then set the full-size tiles in an adjacent quadrant. Set the tiles along the layout lines first, then fill in the interior tiles.

4 To cut tiles that fit against the walls, first lay a tile to be cut so it lines up on top of the last full tile you installed. Then place a 1/8"-thick spacer against the wall. Set a full tile (to use as a marker) up against the spacer so it overlaps the tile to be cut. Trace along the edge of the marker tile to draw a cutting line. The uncovered portion of the tile to be cut will be the part you install.

To mark tiles for cutting around outside corners, first make a cardboard template to match the space, with a 1/8" gap along the walls. After cutting the template, check to make sure it fits. Place the template on a tile and trace its outline.

5 Cut the tile to fit, using a straightedge and a utility knife. Hold the straight-edge securely against cutting lines to ensure a straight cut. **OPTION:** To score and cut thick vinyl tiles, use a tile cutter.

6 Install cut tiles next to the walls.

7 Continue installing tile in the remaining working quadrants until the room is completely covered. Check the floor, and if you find loose areas, press down on tiles to bond them to the underlayment. Install metal threshold bars at project borders where new floor joins another floor covering.

How to Install Dry-back Tile

1 Begin applying adhesive around the intersection of the layout lines, using a trowel with 1/16" V-shaped notches. Hold the trowel at a 45° angle, and spread adhesive evenly over the surface.

2 Spread adhesive over most of the installation area, covering three quadrants. Allow the adhesive to set according to manufacturer's instructions, then begin to install the tile at the intersection of the layout lines. (You can kneel on installed tiles to lay additional tiles.) When one quadrant is completely tiled, spread adhesive over the remaining quadrants, then finish setting the tile.

INSTALLING CERAMIC TILE

Ceramic tile is the hardest and most durable of all surface materials, and is also among the most expensive. (Therefore, choose tiles carefully, avoiding styles that may appear dated in a few years.) Ceramic tiles are installed using a cement-based mortar adhesive and grout to fill the gaps between tiles. These same techniques also are used to install natural stone tiles, like granite and marble. To ensure a long-lasting installation, the best underlayment is cementboard (or the thinner fibre/cementboard), since it is stable and resists moisture. It is ideal for the kitchen and bath. However, in rooms where moisture is not a factor, plywood is an adequate underlayment, and is considerably cheaper.

Ceramic tile includes a wide variety of products made from moulded clay, then baked in a kiln. **Glazed ceramic tile** is coated with a coloured glaze (that protects the porous clay from staining) after it is baked. Then it is fired again to produce a hard surface layer, which is clearly visible when the tile is viewed along the edges. **Quarry tile** is an unglazed, porous tile that is typically softer and thicker than glazed tiles. Unglazed tile should be protected with a sealer after it is installed. **Porcelain tile** is extremely dense and hard, and is naturally water-resistant. Like quarry tiles, porcelain tiles have the same colour throughout their thickness when viewed along the edges. Porcelain tiles are often sold in mosaic sheets with a fibre or paper backing.

Natural-stone tiles are cut from stone extracted from quarries around the world. They are easily identified by visible saw marks at the edges and by their mineral veins or spots. Granite and marble tiles are generally sold with polished and sealed surfaces. Slate tiles are formed by cleaving the stone along natural faults rather than by machine cutting, giving a textured look. Stone tile can be prohibitively expensive for large installations, but can be used economically as an accent in highly visible areas.

Square tiles are commonly available in sizes ranging from 6" to 12". Larger tiles can be installed relatively quickly; they can also make a room look larger. They also have fewer grout lines and are therefore easier to maintain.

Irregular tile shapes include rectangles, hexagons and octagons. Spaces between irregular tiles are often filled with smaller shaped tiles.

Mosaic tiles come in unglazed porcelain and glazed ceramic varieties. They are held together with fibre or paper backing and installed in sheets. Mosaic tiles come in a variety of sizes and shapes; the most common forms are 1" and 2" squares.

Accent tiles, including mosaic borders and painted glazed tiles, are used as borders or placed individually among other tiles.

TIP:
Grout sealers prevent grout joints from trapping dirt and becoming discoloured.

Tiling tools include adhesive-spreading tools, cutting tools and grouting tools. Notched trowels (A) for spreading mortar come with notches of varying sizes and shapes; the size of the notch should be proportional to the size of the tile being installed. Cutting tools include a tile cutter (B), tile nippers (C), hand-held tile cutter (D) and jigsaw with tungsten-carbide blade (E). Grouting tools include a grout float (F), grout sponge (G), buff rag (H) and foam brush (I). Other tiling tools include spacers (J), available in different sizes to create grout joints of varying widths; needlenose pliers (K) for removing spacers; rubber mallet (L) for setting tiles into mortar; and caulk gun (M).

Cutting Tile

Cutting tile accurately takes some practice and patience. Most cutting can be done with a basic tile cutter. Tile cutters come in various configurations; each operates a little differently, though all score and snap tile. Tile stores will often lend cutters to customers.

Tile saws, also called wet saws because they use water to cool blades and tiles, are used primarily for cutting natural-stone tiles. They are also useful for quickly cutting notches in all kinds of hard tile. Wet saws are available for rent at tile dealers and rental shops.

To cut mosaic tiles, use a tile cutter to score tiles in the row where the cut will

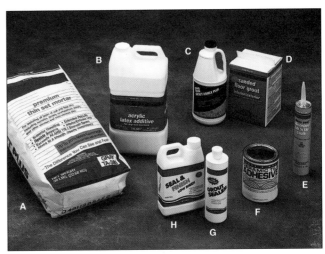

Tile materials include adhesives, grouts and sealers. Thin-set mortar (A), the most common floor-tile adhesive, is often strengthened with latex mortar additive (B). Grout can be made more resilient and durable with grout additive (C). Floor grout (D) is used to fill gaps between tiles; it is available in pre-tinted colours to match your tile. Tile caulk (E) should be used in place of grout where tile meets another surface, like a bathtub. Use wall-tile adhesive (F) for installing base-trim. Grout sealer (G) and porous tile sealer (H) ward off stains and make maintenance easier.

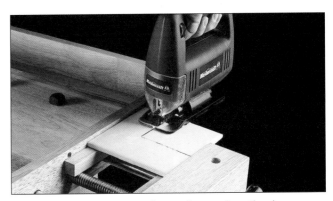

To make square notches, clamp the tile down on a worktable, then use a jigsaw with a tungsten-carbide blade to make the cuts. If you need to cut many notches, rent a wet saw.

occur. Cut away excess strips of mosaics from the sheet, using a utility knife, then use a hand-held tile cutter to snap tiles one at a time. **NOTE:** Use tile nippers to cut narrow portions of tiles after scoring.

- ¼" square-notched trowel
- spade bit
- rubber mallet
- tile cutter
- tile nippers
- hand-held tile cutter
- needlenose pliers
- grout float
- small foam brush

NEEDED MATERIALS

- thin-set mortar
- tile
- tile spacers
- grout
- grout sponge
- soft cloth
- grout sealer
- tile caulk
- threshold material

TIPS:

For large tiles or uneven natural stone, use a larger trowel with notches that are at least ½" deep.

❖❖❖❖❖❖❖❖❖❖❖❖

For mosaic sheets, use a ³⁄₁₆" V-notched trowel to spread mortar.

How to Make Straight Cuts in Ceramic Tile

1 Mark a cutting line on the tile with a pencil, then place the tile in the cutter so the tile-cutting wheel is directly over the line. Pressing down firmly on the wheel handle, run the wheel across the tile to score the surface.

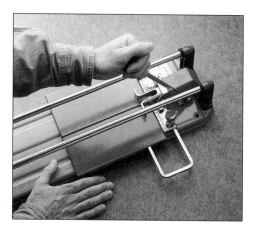

2 Snap the tile along the scored line, as directed by the tool manufacturer. Usually, snapping the tile is accomplished by depressing a lever on the tile cutter (photo above).

How to Make Curved Cuts with Tile Nippers

1 Mark a cutting line on the tile face, then use the scoring wheel of a hand-held tile cutter to score the cut line. Make several parallel scores, not more than ¼" apart, in the waste portion of the tile.

2 Use tile nippers to gradually remove the scored portion of the tile (photo below).
NOTE: To cut circular holes in the middle of a tile, first score and cut the tile so it divides the hole in two, using the straight-cut method, then use the curved-cut method to remove waste material from each half of the hole.

Installing Ceramic Floor Tile

Ceramic tile installations start with the same steps as resilient tile projects: snapping perpendicular layout lines and dry-fitting tiles to ensure the best placement (see pages 20-21).

How to Install Ceramic Tile

1 Draw reference and layout lines, then mix a batch of thin-set mortar. Spread thin-set mortar evenly against both reference lines of one quadrant, using a ¼" square-notched trowel. Use the notched edge of the trowel to create ridges in the mortar bed. Work in small sections so the mortar does not dry before tiles are set. Avoid kneeling on set tiles.

2 Set the first tile in the corner of the quadrant where the reference lines intersect.
NOTE: When setting tiles that are 8" square or larger, twist each tile slightly as you set it into position.

3 Using a soft rubber mallet, gently rap the central area of each tile a few times to set it evenly into the mortar.

4 To ensure consistent spacing between tiles, place plastic tile spacers at corners of the set tile. **NOTE:** With mosaic sheets, use spacers equal to the gaps between tiles so you can space between the sheets properly.

5 Position and set adjacent tiles into mortar along the reference lines. Make sure tiles fit neatly against the spacers.

6 To make sure adjacent tiles are level with one another, lay a straight piece of 2x4 across several tiles at once, and rap the 2x4 with a mallet (photo above).

7 Lay tile in the remaining mortar-covered area. Repeat steps 1 to 6, continuing to work in small sections.

8 Measure and mark tiles for cutting to fit against walls and into corners. Cut tiles to fit. Apply thin-set mortar directly to back of cut tiles, not to the floor, using notched edge of the trowel to furrow the mortar.

9 Set cut pieces into position, and press on them until they are level with adjacent tiles.

10 Measure, cut and install tiles requiring notches or curves to fit around obstacles such as exposed pipes or toilet drains.

11 Carefully remove spacers with needle-nose pliers before mortar hardens.

12 Apply mortar and fill in tiles in remaining quadrants, completing one quadrant at a time.

13 Install threshold material in doorways. If the threshold is too long for the doorway, cut it to fit with a jigsaw or circular saw and a tungsten-carbide blade. Set the threshold in thin-set mortar so the top is even with the tile. Keep the same space between the tiles and threshold as between tiles. Let the mortar cure for at least 24 hours.

14 Prepare a small batch of floor grout to fill tile joints. **NOTE:** When mixing grout for porous tile, such as quarry or natural stone, use an additive with a release agent to prevent grout from bonding to the tile surfaces.

15 Starting in a corner, pour grout over tile. Use a rubber grout float to spread grout outward from corner, pressing firmly on float to completely fill joints. For best results, tilt the float at a 60° angle to the floor and use a figure-eight motion.

16 Use grout float to remove excess grout from surface of tile. Wipe diagonally across the joints, holding the float in a near-vertical position. Continue applying grout and wiping off excess until about 25 sq. ft. of the floor has been grouted.

17 Wipe a damp grout sponge diagonally over about 2 sq. ft. of the tile at a time to remove excess grout. Rinse the sponge in cool water between wipes. Wipe each area once only; repeated wiping can pull grout from the joints. Repeat steps 14 to 17 to apply grout to the rest of the floor.

18 Allow grout to dry for about four hours, then use a soft cloth to buff tile surface free of any grout film.

19 Apply grout sealer to grout lines, using a small foam brush or sash brush. Avoid brushing sealer on tile surfaces. Wipe up any excess sealer immediately. **VARIATION:** Use a tile sealer to seal porous tile, such as quarry tile or any unglazed tile, to protect their surfaces. Roll a thin coat of sealer (refer to manufacturer's instructions) over tile and grout joints with a paint roller and extension handle.

RECOMMENDED HAND TOOLS

- basic hand tools
- carpenter's level
- notched trowel
- tile cutter
- rod saw
- masonry bit
- clamps
- grout float
- small paintbrush
- caulk gun

NEEDED MATERIALS

- straight 1x2
- dry-set tile mortar with latex additive
- ceramic wall tile
- ceramic trim tile
- sponge
- tile grout with latex additive
- tub & tile caulk
- alkaline grout sealer

TIP:

To ensure long-lasting results, remove the old wall surface down to the studs, and install a new base layer of cementboard.

Installing Ceramic Wall Tile

Rows of trimmed tiles (A) *should be positioned near the top and bottom of tiled area to make them less obvious. Layout is adjusted so the row of accent tiles (B) is unbroken by medicine cabinet. Tiles at each end (C) of the same wall should be cut to a similar size. Tiles above tub (D) should be full-size or nearly full-size.*

Ceramic tile is a traditional, custom-installed material often used for kitchen and bath walls and floors. It also is installed on countertops and in bathtub and shower enclosures. Properly installed, ceramic tile outlasts most other wall and floor coverings.

Use a thin layer of dry-set mortar to create a bonding surface for ceramic wall tile. Avoid using the thick beds of standard mortar that were used to set wall tile for so many years. Also avoid adhesives or mastics that have no mortar content, because these products do not work well on vertical surfaces.

Tips for Planning Tile Layouts

Use planning brochures and design catalogues to help you create decorative patterns and borders for your ceramic tile project. Brochures and cata-

logues are available free of charge from many tile manufacturers.

Make a "tile stick" to mark layout patterns on walls. To make a tile stick, set a row of tiles (and plastic spacers, if they will be used) in the selected pattern on a flat surface. Mark a straight 8'-long piece of 1x2 to match the tile spacing. Include any narrow trim tiles or accent tiles. If your tiles are square, you will need only one tile stick. For rectangular and odd-shaped tiles, make separate sticks for the horizontal and vertical layouts.

Ceramic tile types used in bathroom installations include: mosaic tile sheets, 4x4 glazed wall tiles with self-spacing edge lugs, textured quarry tiles (natural stone) for floors, and trim tiles for borders and accents.

How to Mark a Layout for Wall Tile

1 Mark the wall to show planned location of all vanities, wall cabinets, recessed fixtures and ceramic wall accessories, like soap and toothbrush holders or towel rods.

2 Locate the most horizontal line in the bathroom (usually the top edge of the bathtub). Measure up and mark a point at a distance equal to the height of one ceramic tile (if the tub edge is not level, measure up from the lowest spot). Draw a level line through this point, around the entire room. This line represents a tile grout line and is used as a reference line for making the entire tile layout.

3 Use the tile stick to see how the tile pattern will run in relation to other features in the room, like countertops, window and door frames and wall cabinets. Hold the tile stick so it is perpendicular to the horizontal reference line, with one joint mark touching the line, and note the location of tile joints.

4 Adjust the horizontal reference line if the tile stick shows that tile joints will fall in undesirable spots.

5 On each wall, measure and mark the halfway point along the horizontal reference line (photo below). Using the tile stick as a guide, mark lines in each direction from the halfway point to show where the vertical grout joints will be located. If the tile stick shows that the corner tiles will be less than ½ of full tile width, adjust the layout as shown in the next step.

6 Adjust the layout of vertical joints by moving the halfway point (step 5) half the width of a tile in either direction. Use a carpenter's level to draw a vertical reference line through this point, from the floor to the top tile row.

7 Use the tile stick to measure up from the floor along the vertical reference line, a distance equal to the height of one tile plus ⅛", and mark a point on the wall. Draw a level reference line through this point, across the wall.

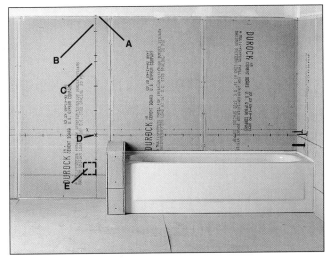

Bullnose border tiles (A), cut tiles (B), *accent tiles (C), starting point (D), cut tiles (E).*

8 Mark reference lines to show where the remaining tile joints will be located, starting at the point where vertical and horizontal reference lines meet. Include any decorative border or accent tiles. If a row of cut tiles is unavoidable, put it near the floor, between the first and third rows, or at the top, near border tiles. Extend horizontal reference lines onto adjoining walls that will be tiled, then repeat steps 5 to 8 for all other walls being tiled.

Halfway point (A), adjusted reference line (B), *original reference line (C).*

How to Install Ceramic Wall Tile

1 Mark layout pattern, then begin installation with the second row of tiles from the floor. If layout requires cut tiles for this row, mark and cut tiles for the entire row.

2 Make straight cuts with a tile cutter. Place the tile face up on the tile cutter, with one side flush against the cutting guide. Adjust the cutting tool to the desired width, then score a groove by pulling the cutting wheel firmly across the tile. Snap the tile along the scored line, as directed by the tool manufacturer.

3 Mix a small batch of dry-set mortar containing a latex additive. (Some mortar has an additive mixed in by the manufacturer, and some mortar must have additive mixed in separately.) Cover the back of the first tile with adhesive, using a 1/4" notched trowel. **ALTERNATE:** Spread adhesive on a small section of the wall, then set the tiles into the adhesive. Dry-set adhesive sets quickly, so work fast if you choose this method.

4 Beginning near the centre of the wall, apply the tile to the wall with a slight twisting motion, aligning it exactly with the horizontal and vertical reference lines.

5 Continue installing tiles, working from the centre to the sides in a pyramid pattern. Make sure to keep tiles aligned with the reference lines. If tiles are not self-spacing, use plastic spacers inserted in the corner joints to maintain even grout lines. The base row should be the last row of full tiles installed.

6 Make notches and curved cuts in tile (photo above right) by clamping the tile to a flat surface, then cutting it with a rod saw (a specialty saw with an abrasive blade designed for cutting tile). For other saw options, see page 23.

7 As small sections of tile are completed, "set" the tile by laying a scrap 2x4 wrapped with carpet onto the tile and tapping it lightly with a mallet. This embeds the tile solidly in the adhesive and creates a flat, even surface.

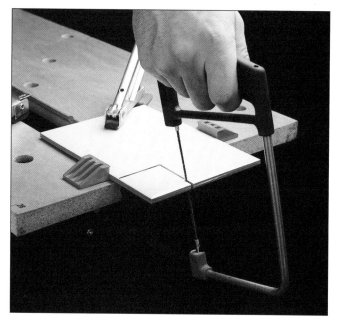

8 To mark tiles for straight cuts, begin by taping 1/8" spacers against the surfaces below and to the side of the tile. Position a tile directly over the last full tile installed, then place a third tile so the edge butts against the spacers. Trace the edge of the top tile onto the middle tile to mark it for cutting.

9 Cut holes for plumbing stub-outs by marking the outline of the hole on the tile, then drilling around the edges of the outline, using a ceramic tile bit (photo below). Gently knock out the waste material with a hammer. Rough edges of the hole

will be covered by protective plates on the fixtures (called escutcheons).

10 Install trim tiles, such as the bullnose edge tiles, at border areas. Wipe away excess mortar along top edge of edge tiles.

11 Use single bullnose and double bullnose tiles at outside corners to cover the rough edges of the adjoining tiles (photo above).

12 Install ceramic accessories by applying dry-set mortar to the back side, then pressing the accessory into place. Use masking tape to hold the accessory in place until the adhesive dries.

13 Let mortar dry completely (12 to 24 hours), then mix a batch of grout containing latex additive. Apply grout with a rubber grout float, using a sweeping motion to force it deep into the joints. Do not grout the joints along the bathtub, floor and room corners. These expansion joints will be caulked instead.

14 Wipe away excess grout with a damp sponge, then dress the grout lines by drawing a small dowel along all joints.

15 When grout is completely hardened, brush alkaline sealer onto the joints with a small paintbrush. Alkaline sealers are better than silicone products for preventing stains and mildew.

16 Seal expansion joints around the bathtub, floor and room corners with tub & tile caulk. After caulk dries, buff tile with a dry, soft cloth.

CABINETS

Cabinets determine how a kitchen looks and functions. Cabinets should provide adequate storage and have a pleasing appearance that harmonizes with other elements in the kitchen and home.

Painting Cabinets

Paint cabinets to renew your kitchen quickly and inexpensively. Cabinets receive heavy use and are frequently scrubbed, so paint them with heavy-duty gloss enamel. Enamel paint is more durable than flat wall paint. Sand surfaces lightly between coats. Varnished cabinets can be painted if the surface is properly prepared. Use liquid deglosser to dull the shine, then prime all surfaces. Alkyd paints work best for painting varnished cabinets. Wood, metal and previously painted cabinets may be painted any colour. Do not paint plastic laminate.

How to Paint Cabinets

1 Empty cabinets. Remove doors, drawers, removable shelves and all hardware. If hardware is to be repainted, strip old paint by soaking hardware in paint remover.

2 Wash cabinets with mild detergent or TSP (trisodium phosphate). Scrape loose paint. Sand all surfaces (photo below). Wipe away sanding dust and prime all bare wood with sealer.

3 Paint interiors first, in this order: 1) back walls, 2) tops, 3) sides, 4) bottoms. Paint bottoms, tops and edges of shelves last.

4 Paint large outside surfaces using a short-nap roller. Work from the top down.

5 Paint both sides of the doors, beginning with inner surfaces. With panel doors, paint in this order: 1) recessed panels, 2) horizontal rails, 3) vertical stiles.

6 Paint drawer fronts last. Let doors and drawers dry several days, then install hardware and hang doors.

Refacing Cabinets

Reface existing kitchen cabinets for a dramatic change in style. Refacing kits include new doors, drawer fronts and veneer for resurfacing cabinet face frames and sides (photo right). Replacement hardware can also be ordered. Contact your local hardware store for information on companies that specialize in refacing cabinets. They come to your home and finish the job within a day. If your existing cabinets are solid, refacing is ideal because it keeps the job cost low.

Selecting New Cabinets

Kitchen cabinets come in a wide array of shapes and finishes, but their basic construction is similar. Traditional-looking **framed cabinets** have cabinet openings that are completely surrounded by face frames made of vertical stiles and horizontal rails, and door hinges are attached directly to the frame. **Frameless cabinets** (also called "European-style") have no face frames. Special "invisible" hinges attach to the inside walls of the cabinet. The doors and drawers on frameless cabinets cover the entire unit. **Modular cabinets** have finished panels on both sides and can be arranged in a variety of ways to fit any kitchen layout. Modular cabinet doors can be reversed to open from either left or right.

TIP:

Built-in cabinets and countertops are usually not salvageable. Cut them into manageable pieces with a Mastercraft reciprocating saw (photo right), or take them apart piece by piece with a hammer and pry bar.

Removing Trim & Old Cabinets

Old cabinets can be salvaged if they are modular units that were installed with screws. Built-in cabinets should be cut to pieces and discarded.

How to Remove Trim

1 Remove trim mouldings at edges and tops of cabinets with a flat pry bar or putty knife.

2 Remove vinyl base trim. Work a pry bar or putty knife underneath and peel off vinyl.

3 Remove baseboards and base shoe mouldings with a pry bar. Protect wall surfaces with scraps of wood.

4 Remove valances. Some are attached to cabinets or soffits with screws. Others are nailed and must be pried loose.

How to Remove Cabinets

1 Remove doors and drawers. You may need to scrape away old paint to expose hinge screws.

2 Remove any screws holding cabinet to wall. Cabinets can be removed as a group, or they can be disassembled.

3 Detach individual cabinets by removing screws that hold face frames together.

- basic hand tools
- pry bar
- putty knife
- straightedge
- level
- stud finder
- trowel
- screwdriver bits

NEEDED MATERIALS

- 1x3 boards, straight 6'-8' long 2x4
- wallboard compound
- 2½" wallboard screws

TIP:

To aid in accuracy when installing wall cabinets, use Mastercraft's hammer drill with built-in level.

Preparing for New Cabinets

Installing new cabinets is easiest if the kitchen is completely empty. Disconnect the plumbing and wiring, and temporarily remove the appliances. Any plumbing or electrical changes should occur now. New flooring should be done before cabinet installation.

How to Prepare Walls

1 Find high and low spots on wall surfaces, using a long, straight 2x4. Sand high spots.

2 Fill in low spots of wall. Apply wallboard taping compound with a trowel. Let dry, and sand lightly.

3 Locate and mark wall studs, using an electronic stud finder. Cabinets will be hung by driving screws into the studs through the back of the cabinets.

High point (A).

4 Find high point along the floor area that will be covered by base cabinets. Place a level on a long, straight 2x4, and move board across floor to determine if floor is uneven. Mark wall at the high point.

5 Measure up 34½" from the high-point mark. Use a level to mark a reference line on walls. Base cabinets will be installed with top edges flush against this line.

6 Measure up 84" from the high-point mark and draw a second reference line (photo below). Wall cabinets will be installed with top edges flush against this line.

7 Measure down 30" from wall-cabinet reference line and draw another level line where bottom of cabinets will be.

8 Install a 1x3 with the top edge flush against this reference line. This will be a temporary ledger (support ledge) that will help position the cabinets during installation. Attach temporary ledgers with 2½" wallboard screws driven into every other wall stud. Mark all stud locations on ledgers.

Installing Cabinets

Cabinets must be firmly anchored to wall studs and must be exactly plumb and level, so that the doors and drawers operate smoothly. Number each cabinet, and mark its position on the wall. Remove the cabinet doors and drawers, and number them so they can be easily replaced after the cabinets are installed.

Fitting a Blind Corner Cabinet

A blind corner cabinet has one end that is tucked behind the cabinets on the adjoining wall. Before installation, test-fit blind corner and adjoining cabinets to make sure doors and handles do not interfere with each other. If necessary, increase the clearance by pulling the blind cabinet away from side wall by no more than 4". For even spacing between edges of doors and the cabinet corner, cut a filler strip and attach it to adjoining cabinet.

How to Install Wall Cabinets

1 Position corner cabinet on ledger (photo above). Drill 3/16" pilot holes into studs through hanging strips at rear of cabinet. Attach to wall with 2½" sheetmetal screws without tightening fully.

2 Attach filler strip (A) to adjoining cabinet (B), if needed (photo above right). Clamp filler in place, and drill pilot holes through cabinet face frame near hinge locations, using a counterbore bit. Attach filler to cabinet with 2½" sheetmetal screws.

3 Position adjoining cabinet on ledger, tight against blind corner cabinet. Check face frame for plumb. Drill 3/16" pilot holes into wall studs through hanging strips in rear of cabinet. Attach cabinet with 2½" sheetmetal screws without tightening fully.

4 Clamp corner cabinet and adjoining cabinet together at the top and bottom.

5 Attach blind corner cabinet to adjoining cabinet. From inside corner cabinet, drill pilot holes through face frame. Join cabinets with sheetmetal screws.

6 Position and attach each additional cabinet. Clamp frames together, and drill counterbored pilot holes through side of face frame. Join cabinets with sheetmetal screws. Drill 3/16" pilot holes in hanging strips, and attach cabinet to studs with sheetmetal screws.

7 Join frameless cabinets with No. 8 gauge 1¼" wood screws and finish washers. Each pair of cabinets should be joined by at least four screws.

8 Fill small spaces between cabinet and a wall or appliance with a filler strip. Cut filler to fit space, then wedge filler into place with wood shims. Drill counterbored pilot holes through side of cabinet face frame, and attach filler with sheetmetal screws.

9 Remove temporary ledger. Check cabinet run for plumb, and adjust if necessary by placing wood shims behind cabinet, near stud locations. Tighten wall screws completely. Cut off shims with utility knife.

10 Use trim mouldings to cover any gaps between cabinets and walls. Stain mouldings to match cabinet finish.

OPTION: Attach decorative valance above sink. Clamp valance to edge of cabinet frames, and drill counterbored pilot holes through cabinet frames into end of valance (similar to method for attaching filler strip). Attach with sheetmetal screws.

11 Install the cabinet doors. Adjust the hinges if doors are not straight and plumb.

TIP:

Make sure cabinet is plumb and level. Use a Mastercraft level often to check your accuracy. If necessary, adjust by driving wood shims under cabinet base. Be careful not to damage flooring.

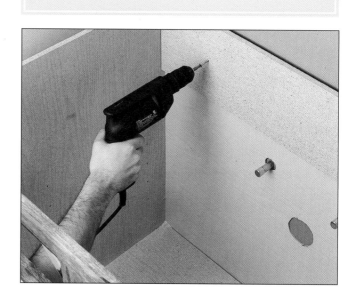

How to Install Base Cabinets

1 Use a jigsaw to cut cabinet openings needed for plumbing, wiring or heating ducts (photo above).

2 Begin installation with corner cabinet. Position cabinet so that top is flush with reference line. Drill 3/16" pilot holes through hanging strip into wall studs. Attach cabinets loosely to wall with sheetmetal screws (photo above right).

3 Attach filler strip to adjoining cabinet, if necessary. Clamp filler in place, and drill counterbored pilot holes through

side of face frame. Attach filler with sheetmetal screws.

4 Clamp adjoining cabinet to corner cabinet. Make sure cabinet is plumb, then drill counterbored pilot holes through corner-cabinet face frame into filler strip. Join cabinets with sheetmetal screws. Drill 3/16" pilot holes through hanging strips into wall studs. Attach cabinets loosely with sheetmetal screws.

5 Position and attach additional cabinets, making sure frames are aligned. Clamp cabinets together, then drill counterbored pilot holes through side of face frame. Join cabinets with sheetmetal screws. Frameless cabinets are joined with No. 8 gauge 1¼" wood screws and finish washers.

6 Make sure all cabinets are level. If necessary, adjust by driving wood shims underneath cabinets. Place wood shims behind cabinets near stud locations wherever there is a gap. Tighten wall screws. Cut off shims with a utility knife.

7 Use trim mouldings to cover gaps between the cabinets and the wall or floor. Toe-kick area is often covered with a strip of hardwood finished to match the cabinets (photo below left).

8 If corner has a void area not covered by cabinets, screw 1x3 cleats to wall, flush with reference line. Cleats will help support countertop.

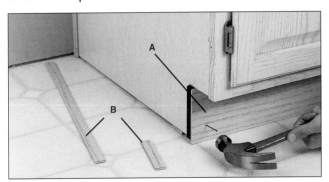

***Trim moulding (A)**, shims (B).*

How to Install a Ceiling-hung Cabinet to Joists

1 Cut a cardboard template to the same size as top of wall cabinet. Use a template to outline the position of cabinet on ceiling. Mark position of the cabinet face frame on the outline.

2 Locate joists with stud finder. If joists run parallel to cabinet, install blocking between joists to hang cabinet. Measure joist positions and mark cabinet frame to indicate where to drive screws.

3 Have one or more helpers position cabinet against ceiling. Drill ³⁄₁₆" pilot holes through top rails into ceiling joists. Attach cabinets with 4" wood screws and finish washers.

How to Install a Base Island Cabinet

1 Set the base cabinet in the correct position, and lightly trace the cabinet outline on the flooring. Remove the cabinet.

2 Attach L-shaped 2x4 cleats to floor at opposite corners of cabinet outline. Allow for thickness of cabinet walls by positioning cleats ¾" inside cabinet outline. Attach cleat to floor with 3" wallboard screws.

3 Lower the base cabinet over the cleats. Check cabinet for level, and shim under the base, if necessary.

4 Attach the cabinet to the floor cleats using 6d finish nails. Drill plot holes for nails, and recess nail heads with a nail set.

Blocking (A).

How to Attach a Ceiling-hung Cabinet to Blocking (joists must be accessible)

1 Drill reference holes through the ceiling at each corner of cabinet outline. From above ceiling, install 2x4 blocks between joists. Blocking can be toenailed, or end-nailed through joists (photo above right).

2 Measure distance between each block and the drilled reference holes. Mark cabinet frame to indicate where to drive anchoring screws. Drill pilot holes and attach cabinet to blocking with 4" wood screws and finish washers.

Installing Cabinets in Your Bathroom

When installing cabinets in damp locations, like a bathroom, choose the best cabinets you can afford. Look for quality indicators, like dowelled construction, hardwood doors and drawers, and high-gloss, moisture-resistant finishes. Avoid cabinets with sides or doors that are painted on one side and finished with laminate or veneer on the other, because these cabinets are more likely to warp.

How to Install a Surface-mounted Cabinet

1 Locate wall studs and mark them clearly on the wall surface. Draw a level line at the desired top height of the cabinet body, then measure and mark a second line to indicate the bottom of the cabinet.

2 Attach a temporary ledger board (usually 1x4) just below the lower level line, using duplex nails. Nail holes can be patched with wallboard compound after the cabinet installation is completed.

3 Rest the base of the cabinet on the ledger, and hold it in place, or brace it with 2x4s. Attach the cabinet to the wall at stud locations by drilling pilot holes and driving wood screws. Remove ledger when finished.

> **TIP:**
> Make sure to wear eye, ear and mouth protection while using the Mastercraft circular saw.

How to Install a Recessed Bath Cabinet

1 Locate the first stud beyond either side of planned cabinet location, then remove wall surface between these studs. (Removing wall surface all the way to the ceiling simplifies patching work.) Cut along the centre of studs, using a circular saw with blade depth set to equal thickness of wall surface (photo below).

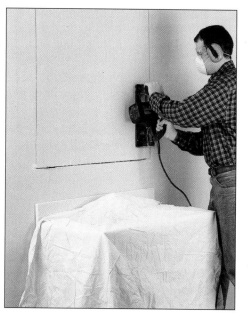

2 Mark a rough opening ½" taller than cabinet frame onto the exposed wall studs. Add 1½" for each header and sill plate, then cut out studs in rough opening area.

3 Frame out the top and bottom of the rough opening by installing a header and a sill plate between the cut wall studs. Make sure the header and sill plate are level, then nail them in place with 10d common nails.

4 Mark the rough opening width on the header and sill plates, centring the opening over the sink. Cut and nail jack studs between the header and the sill plate, just outside the rough opening marks.

NOTE: Do any wiring work for light fixtures, then install new wall surface before proceeding.

5 Position the cabinet in the opening. Check it for level with a carpenter's level, then attach the cabinet by drilling pilot holes and driving wood screws through the top and bottom of the cabinet sides and into the wall studs, header and sill plate. Attach doors, shelves and hardware.

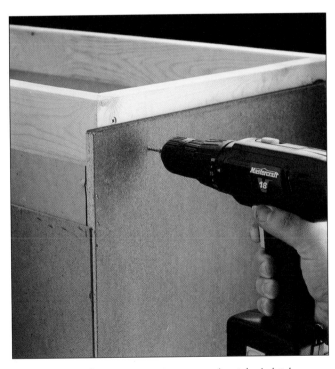

Raise a vanity to a more convenient height by attaching an extension made of 2x4s to the base of the vanity. Attach the extension by screwing through the cabinet sides and into the 2x4s.

How to Install a Vanity

1 Mark the top edge of the vanity cabinet on the wall. Using a carpenter's level, draw a level line at the cabinet height.

2 Slide the vanity into position. The back of the cabinet should be flush against the wall. (If the wall surface is uneven, position the vanity so it contacts the wall in at least one spot and the back cabinet rail is parallel with the wall.)

3 Shim below the vanity until it is level, using the line on the wall as a guide.

4 Locate wall studs, then drive 2½" wallboard screws through the rail on the cabinet back and into wall studs. Screws should be driven at both corners and in the centre of the back rail.

5 Attach any trim and moulding required to cover the gaps between the vanity and the wall, and between the vanity and the floor. (Small gaps may be filled with caulk instead.)

Installation Variations

Two or more cabinets: Set the cabinets in position against the wall, and align the cabinet fronts. If one cabinet is higher than the other, shim under the lower cabinet until the two cabinets are even. Clamp the cabinet faces together, then drill countersunk pilot holes through the face frames, spaced 12" apart, at least halfway into the face frame of the second cabinet. Drive wood screws through the pilot holes to join the cabinets together.

Vanities with backs: Mark a line on the wall where the top of vanity will fit, then draw a line down the wall from the midpoint of this line. Draw a corresponding centreline down the back of the vanity. Measure the distance from the supply and drain pipes to the centreline on the wall. Transfer distances to the back of the vanity, measuring from the centreline. Mark pipe cut-outs, then cut with a hole saw or a jigsaw.

COUNTERTOPS

Countertops provide the main workspace in a kitchen or bathroom, so they must be made from durable and easy-to-clean materials. Countertops add colour, pattern, texture and shape to kitchens and baths, so choose a style that harmonizes with the other elements in the room.

Post-form countertops are made of sheet laminates glued to particleboard and come from the factory ready to install. Post-form countertops have pre-attached backsplashes and front edge treatments. They are manufactured in a variety of colours and styles, and are often used in the bathroom.

Custom laminate countertops are built by gluing sheet laminates to particleboard. Laminates are available in hundreds of colours and patterns to match any kitchen decorating scheme. Special edge treatments can be added to customize a laminate countertop.

Ceramic tile is especially durable and creates a beautiful surface that resists spills and stains. Tile is available in a wide range of styles and prices, and creating a ceramic tile countertop is an excellent do-it-yourself project. Ceramic tile is commonly used for bathroom countertops and is installed using the same methods as for floor and wall installations (see pages 22 and 26).

Solid-surface materials are manufactured from acrylic or polyester resins mixed with additives and formed into sheets that are ¼", ½" or ¾" thick. Solid-surface materials are expensive, but they are tough and easy to maintain. They can be cut and shaped with woodworking tools.

Integral sink-countertops are made in standard sizes to fit common vanity widths in the bathroom. Because the sink and countertop are cast from the same material, integral sink-countertops do not leak and do not require extensive caulking and sealing.

How to Remove an Old Countertop

1 Turn off water at shutoff valves. Disconnect and remove plumbing fixtures and appliances. Remove any brackets or screws holding the countertop to the cabinets. Unscrew the take-up bolts on mitred countertops.

2 Use a utility knife to cut caulk beads along backsplash and edge of countertop. Remove any trim. Using a flat pry bar, try to lift countertop away from base cabinets.

3 If countertop cannot be pried up, use a reciprocating saw or jigsaw with coarse wood-cutting blade to cut the countertop into pieces for removal. Be careful not to cut into base cabinets.

TIP:

When removing ceramic tile, always wear eye protection. Chisel tile away from the base with a masonry chisel and Mastercraft ball peen hammer. A tile countertop that has a mortar bed can be cut into pieces with a Mastercraft circular saw using an abrasive masonry-cutting blade.

RECOMMENDED POWER TOOLS

JIGSAW

CIRCULAR SAW

DRILL

• belt sander

RECOMMENDED HAND TOOLS

- basic hand tools
- framing square
- straightedge
- C-clamps
- spade bit
- level
- caulk gun
- file
- adjustable wrench
- scribing compass
- J-roller

NEEDED MATERIALS

- post-form countertop sections
- wood shims
- take-up bolts
- wallboard screws
- wire brads
- household iron
- endcap laminate
- endcap battens
- silicone caulk
- carpenter's glue
- build-up blocks

How to Install a Post-form Countertop

1 Measure span of base cabinets, from corner to outside edge of cabinet. Add 1" for overhang if end will be exposed. If an end will butt against an appliance, subtract 1/16" to prevent scratches.

2 Use a framing square to mark a cutting line on the bottom surface of the countertop. Cut off the countertop with a jigsaw, using a clamped straightedge as a guide.

3 Attach battens from endcap kit to edge of countertop, using carpenter's glue and small brads (photo above right). Sand out any unevenness with belt sander.

4 Hold endcap laminate against end, slightly overlapping edges. Activate adhesive by pressing an iron set at medium heat against endcap. Cool with wet cloth, then file endcap laminate flush with edges.

5 Position countertop on base cabinets. Make sure front edge of countertop is parallel to cabinet face. Check countertop for level. Make sure that drawers and doors open and close freely. If needed, adjust countertop with wood shims.

Scribing strip (A).

6 Because walls are usually uneven, use a compass to trace wall outline onto backsplash scribing strip (photo left). Set compass arms to match widest gap, then move compass along length of the wall to transfer outline to scribing strip.

7 Remove countertop. Use belt sander to grind backsplash to scribe line (photo below).

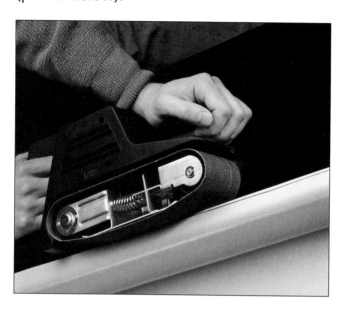

8 Mark cut-out for self-rimming sink. Position sink upside down on countertop and trace outline. Remove sink and draw cutting line 5⁄8" inside sink outline.

9 Mark cut-out for a cooktop (a cooking unit that is set into a countertop) or sink with a frame. Position cooktop or frame on countertop, mark outline around the innermost edge where it touches the countertop, then remove it.

10 Drill pilot hole just inside cutting line. Make cut-outs with jigsaw. Support cut-out area from below so that falling cut-out does not damage cabinet.

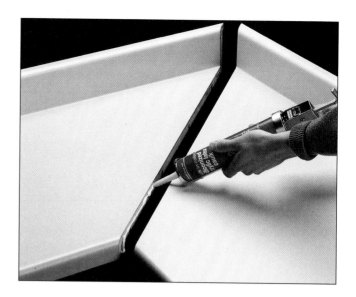

11 Apply a bead of silicone caulk on edges of mitred countertop sections (photo above). Force countertop pieces tightly together.

12 From underneath cabinet, install and tighten mitre take-up bolts (photo below). Position countertop tightly against wall and fasten to cabinets by driving wallboard screws up through corner brackets into the countertop. Screws should be long enough to provide maximum holding power, but not long enough to puncture laminate surface.

13 Seal seam between backsplash and wall with silicone caulk. Smooth bead with a wet fingertip. Wipe away excess caulk.

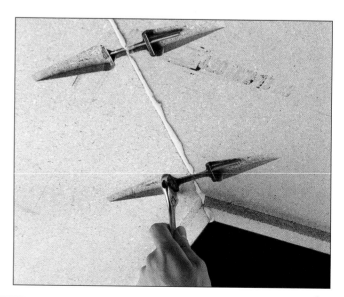

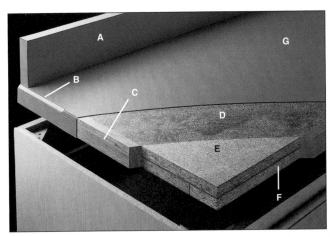

Laminate countertop: *Laminate pieces are bonded to the countertop with contact cement. The countertop core is ³⁄₄" particleboard. Perimeter is built up with strips of particleboard screwed to the bottom of the core. For decorative edge treatments, hardwood strips can be attached to the core. The edges are trimmed and shaped with a router. Backsplash (A), shaped edge (B), hardwood strip (C), contact cement (D), particleboard core (E), build-up strip (F), laminate (G).*

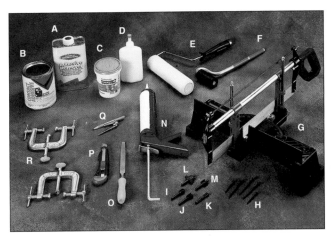

Specialty tools & materials: *contact cement thinner (A), contact cement (B), latex wood patch (C), carpenter's glue (D), paint roller (E), J-roller (F), Mastercraft mitre box (G), wallboard screws (H), round-nose router bit (I), 15° bevel-cutting router bit (J), straight router bit (K), corner-rounding router bit (L), rabbeting router bit (M), silicone caulk (N), file (O), scoring tool (P), scribing compass (Q), 3-way clamps (R).*

How to Build a Custom Laminate Countertop

1 Measure along tops of base cabinets to determine size of countertop. If wall corners are not square, use a framing square to establish a reference line near middle of base cabinets, perpendicular to front of cabinets. Take four measurements from reference line to cabinet ends. Allow for overhangs by adding 1" to the length for each exposed end and 1" to the width. If an end butts against an appliance, subtract ¹⁄₁₆" from length to prevent scratching appliance.

2 Cut core to size, using a circular saw with clamped straightedge as a guide. Cut 4" strips of particleboard for backsplash and for joint support where sections of the core are butted together. Cut 3" strips for edge build-ups.

3 Join the countertop core pieces on the bottom side. Attach a 4" particleboard joint support across the seam, using carpenter's glue and 1¼" wallboard screws.

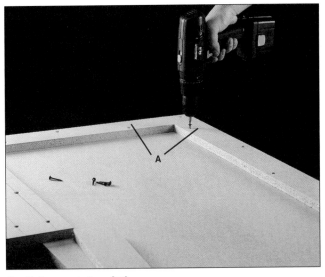

Build-up strips (A).

4 Attach 3" edge build-up strips to bottom of countertop, using 1¼" wallboard screws (photo above). Fill any gaps on outside edges with latex wood patch, then sand edges with belt sander.

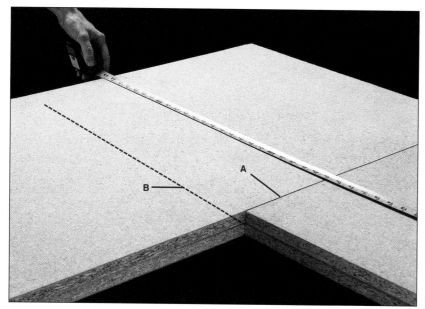

Core seam (A), *laminate seam (B).*

5 To determine the size of the laminate top, measure countertop core. For strength, laminate seams should run opposite to core seam (photo above). Add ½" trimming margin to both the length and width of each piece. Measure laminate needed for face and edges of backsplash, and for exposed edges of countertop core. Add ½" to each measurement.

6 Cut laminate by scoring twice and breaking it. Draw a cutting line, then etch along the line with a scoring tool. Use a straightedge as a guide.

7 Bend laminate toward the scored line until the sheet breaks cleanly. For better control on narrow pieces, clamp a straightedge along scored line before bending laminate.

TIP:

Choose non-flammable contact cement when building a laminate countertop, and thoroughly ventilate your work area. Wear gloves to avoid being cut by sharp laminate edges.

8 Create tight-fitting seams with plastic laminate by using a router and a straight bit to trim edges that will butt together. Measure from cutting edge of the bit to edge of the router baseplate. Place laminate on scrap wood and align edges. To guide the router, clamp a straightedge on the laminate at distance A plus ⅛", parallel to laminate edge. Trim laminate.

9 Apply laminate to sides of countertop first. Using a paint roller, apply two coats of contact cement to edge of countertop and one coat to back of laminate. Let cement dry according to manufacturer's directions. Position laminate carefully, then press against edge of countertop. To ensure a good bond, roll with J-roller.

10 Use a router and flush-cutting bit to trim edge strip flush with top and bottom surfaces of countertop core. At edges where router cannot reach, trim excess laminate with a file. Apply laminate to remaining edges, and trim with router.

11 Test-fit laminate top on countertop core. Check that laminate overhangs all edges. At seam locations, draw a reference line on core where laminate edges will butt together. Remove laminate. Make sure all surfaces are free of dust, then apply one coat of contact cement to back of laminate and two coats to core. Place spacers made of ¼"-thick scrap wood at 6" intervals across countertop core. Because contact cement bonds instantly,

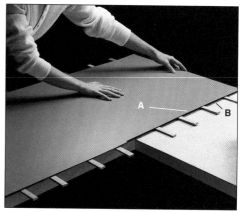

Trimmed edge (A), *reference line (B).*

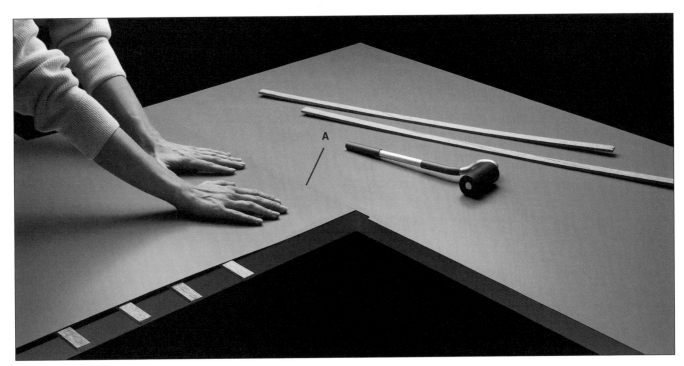

Butt seam (A).

spacers allow laminate to be positioned accurately over core without bonding. Align laminate with seam reference line (photo opposite page, bottom). Beginning at one end, remove spacers and press laminate to countertop core.

12 Apply contact cement to remaining core and next piece of laminate. Let cement dry, then position laminate on spacers, and carefully align butt seam. Beginning at seam edge, remove spacers pressing laminate to the core (photo above).

13 Roll entire surface with J-roller to bond laminate to core. Clean off any excess contact cement with a soft cloth and contact cement thinner.

14 Remove excess laminate with a router and flush-cutting bit. At edges where router cannot reach, trim excess laminate with a file.

15 Finish-trim the edges with a router and 15° bevel-cutting bit. Set bit depth so that bevel edge is cut only on top laminate layer. Bit should not cut into vertical edge surface. Use file where router cannot reach.

16 File all edges smooth. Use downward file strokes to avoid chipping the laminate.

17 Cut 1¼"-wide strips of ¼" plywood to form overhanging scribing strip for backsplash core with glue and wallboard screws. Cut laminate pieces and apply to exposed sides, top and front of backsplash. Trim each piece as it is applied.

18 Test-fit countertop and backsplash. Because walls may be uneven, use compass to trace wall outline onto backsplash scribing strip. Use a belt sander to grind backsplash to scribe line.

19 Apply a bead of silicone caulk to the bottom edge of the backsplash.

20 Position the backsplash on the countertop, and clamp it into place with bar clamps. Wipe away excess caulk, and let dry.

21 Screw 2" wallboard screws through countertop into backsplash core. Make sure screwheads are countersunk completely for a tight fit against the base cabinet.

Make final connections for faucets, drains and appliances after an electrician or plumber has finished the rough work. A licensed plumber or electrician will make sure the job conforms to local Codes (see pages 10-11).

Where Codes allow, have the electrician install plug-in outlets for all major appliances. This makes it easy to disconnect the appliances for servicing.

- caulk gun
- hacksaw
- tubing cutter
- hole saw
- groove joint pliers
- hose clamps
- combination tool
- Robo-Grip pliers/adjustable wrench

NEEDED MATERIALS

- sink frame
- mounting clips
- plumber's putty
- silicone caulk

Installing a Kitchen Sink

Kitchen sinks for do-it-yourself installation are made from cast iron coated with enamel, stainless steel or enamelled steel.

Cast-iron sinks are heavy, durable and relatively easy to install. Most cast-iron sinks are frameless, requiring no mounting hardware.

Stainless steel and enamelled steel sinks weigh less than cast iron. They may require a metal frame and mounting brackets. A good stainless steel sink is made of heavy 18- or 20-gauge nickel steel, which holds up well under use. Lighter steel (designated by numbers higher than 20) dents easily.

Some premium-quality sinks are made from solid-surface material or porcelain and are usually installed by professionals.

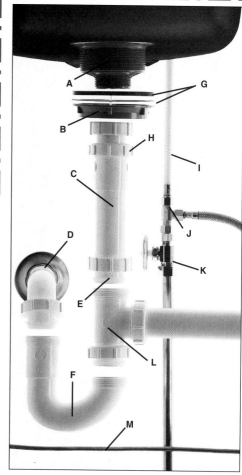

Strainer (A), *locknut (B), tailpiece (C), trap arm (D), bevelled washer (E), trap bend (F), washers (G), slip nut (H), hot water supply tube (I), T-fitting (J), hot water shutoff (K), continuous waste-T (L), copper tubing to refrigerator icemaker (M).*

TIP:

If a remodelling job requires new plumbing and wiring, the work should be completed in the early stage of the project, before new flooring, cabinets or appliances are installed.

How to Install a Frameless Sink

1 After making the counter-top cut-out, lay the sink upside down. Apply a ¼" bead of silicone caulk or plumber's putty around the underside of sink flange (photo right).

2 Position front of sink in the countertop cut-out, by holding it from the drain openings. Carefully lower the sink into position. Press down to create a tight seal, then wipe away excess caulk.

How to Install a Framed Sink

1 Turn the sink frame upside down. Apply a ¼" bead of silicone caulk or plumber's putty around both sides of the vertical flange.

2 Set the sink upside down inside the frame. Bend frame tabs to hold the sink. Carefully set the sink into the cut-out opening, and press down to create a tight seal.

3 Hook mounting clips every 6" to 8" around the frame from underneath countertop (photo right). Tighten mounting screws. Wipe away excess caulk from the frame.

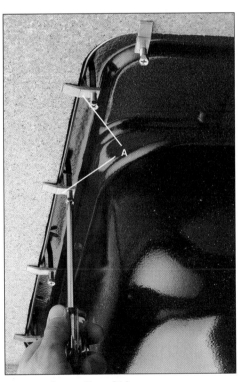

Mounting clips (A).

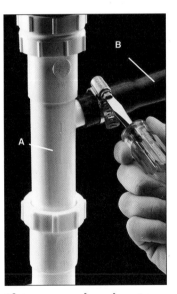

If you are planning to install a dishwasher, attach a special waste-T sink tailpiece to sink strainer. Attach the drain hose to the waste-T nipple with a hose clamp (see pages 52-53). Then attach waste-T tail piece (A), to dishwasher (B).

TIP:
When choosing a sink, make sure the pre-drilled openings will fit your faucet.

MASTERCRAFT

BASIC HAND TOOLS

- scissors
- carpenter's level
- groove joint pliers
- ratchet wrench
- basin wrench

NEEDED MATERIALS

- cardboard
- plumber's putty
- lag screws
- tub & tile caulk

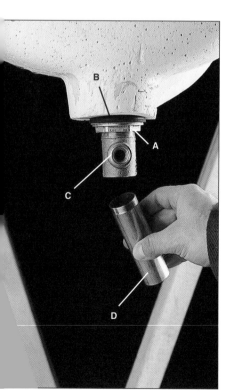

Installing an Integral Sink-Countertop

Generally used in the bathroom, the integral (one-piece) sink-countertop units are made from cultured marble or other solid materials, like Corian® or Swanstone. Integral sink-countertops are convenient, and many are inexpensive, but style and colour options are limited.

How to Install an Integral Sink-Countertop

1 Set sink-countertop onto sawhorses. Attach faucet, and slip the drain lever through the faucet body. Place a ring of plumber's putty around the drain flange, then insert the flange in the drain opening.

2 Thread locknut (A) and sealing gasket (B) onto drain tailpiece (C), then insert tailpiece into drain opening and screw it onto drain flange (photo left). Tighten locknut securely. Attach tailpiece extension (D). Insert pop-up stopper linkage.

3 Apply a layer of tub & tile caulk (or adhesive if specified by the countertop manufacturer) to the top edges of the vanity and to any corner braces.

4 Centre the sink-countertop unit over the vanity, so the overhang is equal on both sides and the backsplash of the countertop is flush with the wall. Press the countertop evenly into the caulk.

5 Attach the drain arm to the drain stub-out, using a slip nut. Attach one end of the P-trap to the drain arm, and the other to the tailpiece of the sink drain, using slip nuts. Connect supply tubes to the faucet tailpieces.

6 Seal the gap between the backsplash and the wall with tub & tile caulk.

How to Install a Pedestal Sink

1 You must install a piece of 2x4 (called blocking) between wall studs positioned so the sink can be attached to it. The face of the 2x4 should be flush with the front edges of the studs. Then cover the wall with water-resistant wallboard.

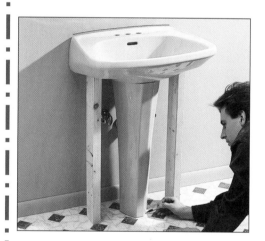

2 Set the basin and pedestal in position, bracing the basin with 2x4s. Outline the top of the basin on the wall, and mark the base of the pedestal on the floor (photo above). Mark reference points on the wall and floor through the mounting holes found on the back of the sink and the bottom of the pedestal.

3 Set aside the basin and pedestal. Drill pilot holes in the wall and floor at reference points, then reposition the pedestal. Anchor the pedestal to the floor with lag screws.

4 Attach the faucet, then set the sink on the pedestal. Align the holes in the back of the sink with the pilot holes drilled in the wall, then drive lag screws and washers into the wall brace, using a ratchet wrench. Do not overtighten.

5 Hook up the drain and supply fittings. Caulk between the back of the sink and the wall when installation is finished.

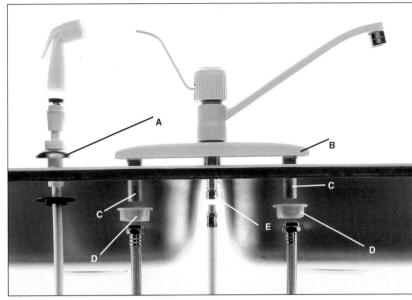

Faucet and drain systems consist of: sprayer base (A), optional, generally used in kitchens; faucet base (B); tailpiece (C); mounting nut (D); hose stub-out (E).

Installing a Faucet & Drain

Connect the faucet to hot and cold water lines with easy-to-install flexible supply tubes made from vinyl or braided steel.

Where local Codes allow, use plastic piping for drain hook-ups. Plastic is inexpensive and easy to install. A wide selection of extensions and angle fittings let you easily plumb any sink configuration. Manufacturers offer kits that contain all the fittings needed for attaching a food disposer or dishwasher to the sink drain system.

TIP:
Keep Mastercraft groove joint pliers or Robo-Grip pliers nearby when installing your faucet and drain. They are an integral part of the installation process.

How to Install a Faucet & Drain

1 Apply a ¼" bead of plumber's putty or silicone caulk around base of faucet. Apply putty around base of sprayer mount.

2 Insert faucet and sprayer tailpieces into sink openings. Screw mounting nuts onto tailpieces and tighten them securely, using groove joint pliers or basin wrench.

3 Connect supply tubes to faucet tailpieces, using groove joint pliers. Attach sprayer hose to hose stub-out.

4 Connect left supply tube to the hot water shutoff valve, using groove joint pliers.

5 Attach the right supply tube to the cold water shutoff valve, using groove joint pliers.

RECOMMENDED HAND TOOLS

MASTERCRAFT

BASIC HAND TOOLS

- hacksaw
- tubing cutter
- hole saw
- groove joint pliers
- combination tool
- caulk gun

NEEDED MATERIALS

- faucet
- flexible vinyl or braided steel supply tubes
- drain components
- plumber's putty
- silicone caulk
- hose clamps

- basin wrench
- Robo-Grip pliers/adjustable wrench
- groove joint pliers

- plumber's putty
- Teflon® tape
- joint compound

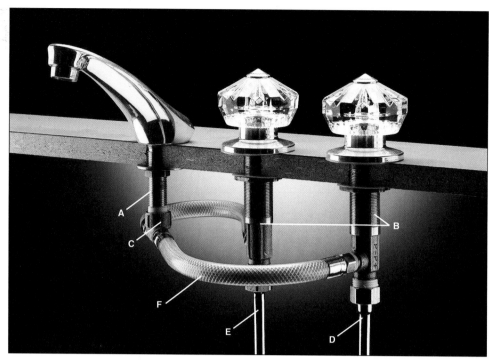

Wide-spread faucets & spouts *consist of: spout tailpiece (A), faucet valves (B), connector-T (C), cold water supply tube (D), hot water supply tube (E), flex tube (F).*

TIP:

Wide-spread faucets are often installed on whirlpools and tubs that are mounted in platforms. Position the handles and spout carefully so that they are not in the way when entering or exiting the tub. They also cannot be used as handles to assist in getting up from the tub.

Installing Bathroom Faucets & Spouts

One-piece faucets, with either one or two handles, are the most popular fixtures for bathroom installations. "Wide-spread" faucets with separate spout and handles are being installed with increasing frequency, however. Because the handles are connected to the spout with flex tubes that can be 18" or longer, wide-spread faucets can be arranged in many ways.

Connecting Supply Tubes & Spouts

Connect supply tubes after the sink and faucet body are installed. Tubes should be slightly longer than the distance from the shutoff valves to the faucet tailpieces. Most tubes have a flared end that fits into the faucet tailpiece. Wrap threads of tailpieces with Teflon tape before attaching tubes.

Connect tub spouts by applying joint compound or Teflon tape to the threaded end of the spout nipple that extends from the wall. Screw the spout onto the nipple, using a long screwdriver as a lever. Some spouts have a setscrew on the underside that must be tightened.

How to Install a Wide-spread Faucet

Drill holes for faucet handles and spout in deck or countertop, according to manufacturer's suggestions. Slide a protective washer onto the spout tailpiece, insert the tailpiece, then insert the tailpiece into the spout hole.

1 From beneath the deck, slide a metal washer onto spout tailpiece, then attach a locknut. Tighten the nut by hand, then check to make sure the spout is properly aligned. Tighten with a basin wrench until snug.

2 Attach faucet valves to deck, using washers and locknuts, as directed by the manufacturer. **NOTE:** Some wide-spread faucet valves, like the one pictured on the opposite page, are inserted up through the hole and have locknuts above and below.

3 Wrap Teflon tape around spout tailpiece, then attach the connector-T to the tailpiece. Attach one end of each flex tube to the T, and the other end to the proper faucet valve. Wrap Teflon tape around faucet valve tailpieces, then attach hot and cold water supply tubes to tailpieces.

4 Attach faucet handle flanges and faucet handles, according to manufacturer's directions. Cover exposed screw heads with trim caps.

How to Install a One-piece Faucet

1 Apply a ring of plumber's putty around the base of the faucet body. (Some faucets use a gasket that does not require plumber's putty – read the manufacturer's directions carefully.)

2 Insert the faucet tailpieces through holes in countertop or sink. From below, thread washers and locknuts over the tailpieces, then tighten the locknuts with a basin wrench until snug.

3 Wrap Teflon tape around the tailpiece threads, then attach the supply tube couplings and tighten until snug. Connect drain linkage, then attach handles and trim caps.

Installing Tub & Shower Faucets

Two-handled faucet: *Screw handle flanges onto faucet valve stems, then attach handles to stems, using mounting screws. Attach spout and trim caps.* ***NOTE:*** *Faucet body is attached before wall surface is installed. Faucet parts: faucet body (A), handle flanges (B), trim cap (C), faucet valve stem (D), spout (E).*

Single-handled faucets: *Open built-in shutoff valves, using a screwdriver, then attach escutcheon plate to faucet body with mounting screws. Attach faucet handle with mounting screw, then attach spout and trim cap.* ***NOTE:*** *Faucet body is attached before wall surface is installed. Faucet parts: built-in shutoff valves (A), faucet body (B), spout (C), escutcheon plate (D), mounting screws (E), faucet handle (F).*

MASTERCRAFT

BASIC HAND TOOLS

- hacksaw
- tubing cutter
- Robo-Grip pliers/adjustable wrench
- groove joint pliers
- tubing bender
- felt-tipped pen

NEEDED MATERIALS

- shutoff valves
- supply tubes
- pipe joint compound

TIPS:

Use the Mastercraft hacksaw when you need to cut old soldered copper pipes that you cannot cut with a tubing cutter.

❖❖❖❖❖❖❖❖❖❖❖❖❖

When attaching supply tubes to shutoff valves, hand-tighten the nuts, then use an adjustable Mastercraft wrench to tighten nuts ¼ turn. If necessary, hold valve with another wrench while tightening.

Connecting a Faucet with Pre-attached Supply Tubing

Attach faucet to sink by placing rubber gasket, retainer ring and locknut onto threaded tailpiece. Tighten locknut with a basin wrench or groove joint pliers. Some centre-mounted faucets have a decorative coverplate. Secure coverplate from underneath with washers and locknuts onto coverplate bolts.

Connect pre-attached supply tubing to shutoff valves with compression fittings. Red-coded tube should be attached to the hot water pipe, blue-coded tube to the cold water pipe.

Installing Shutoff Valves & Supply Tubes

Shutoff valves allow you to shut off the water to an individual fixture so it can be repaired. They can be made from durable chromed brass or lightweight plastic. Shutoff valves come in ½" and ¾" diameters to match common water pipe sizes.

Shutoff valves are available in several fitting types. For copper pipes, valves with compression-type fittings are easiest to install. For plastic pipes, use grip-type valves. For galvanized iron pipes, use valves with female threads.

Worn-out shutoff valves or supply tubes can cause water to

Faucet parts: *washer (A), locknut (B), coverplate bolt (C), tailpiece (D), rubber gasket (E), locknut (F), retainer ring (G).*

leak underneath a sink or other fixture. First, try tightening the fittings with an adjustable wrench. If this does not fix the leak, replace the shutoff valves and supply tubes.

Older plumbing systems often were installed without fixture shutoff valves. When repairing or replacing plumbing fixtures, you may want to install shutoff valves if they are not already present.

Supply tubes are used to connect water pipes to faucets, toilets and other fixtures. They come in 12", 20" and 30" lengths. PB plastic and chromed copper tubes are inexpensive. Braided steel and vinyl mesh supply tubes are easy to install.

How to Install Shutoff Valves & Supply Tubes

1 Turn off water at the main shutoff valve. Remove old supply pipes. If pipes are soldered copper, cut them off just below the soldered joint, using a hacksaw or tubing cutter. Make sure the cuts are straight. Unscrew the coupling nuts, and discard the old pipes.

2 Slide a compression nut and compression ring over copper water pipe. Threads of nut should face end of pipe.

3 Slide shutoff valve onto pipe. Apply a layer of pipe joint compound to compression nut onto the shutoff valve and tighten with an adjustable wrench or Robo-Grip pliers.

4 Bend chromed copper supply tube to reach from the tailpiece of the fixture to the shutoff valve, using a tubing bender. Bend the tube slowly to avoid crimping the metal.

5 Position the supply tube between fixture tailpiece and shutoff valve, and mark tube to length (photo top right). Cut supply tube with a tubing cutter.

6 Attach bell-shaped end of supply tube to fixture tailpiece with coupling nut, then attach other end to shutoff valve with compression ring and nut. Tighten all fittings with an adjustable wrench or Robo-Grip pliers (photo bottom right).

Fixture tailpiece (A), sprayer hose (B), shutoff valve (C), supply tube (D).

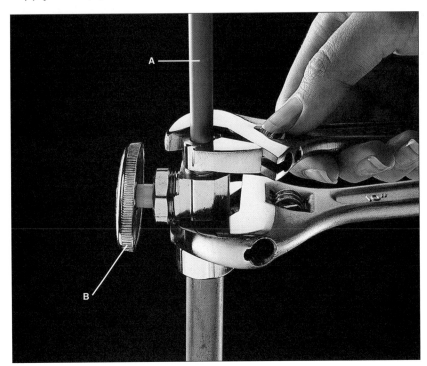

Supply tube (A), shutoff valve (B).

Drain line hookups *consist of: washers (A), strainer (B), locknut (C), insert washer (D), slip nut (E).*

1 Install sink strainer in each sink drain opening. Apply ¼" bead of plumber's putty around bottom of flange. Insert strainer into drain opening. Place rubber and fibre washers over neck of strainer. Screw locknut onto neck and tighten with groove joint pliers.

2 Attach tailpiece to strainer. Place insert washer in flared end of tailpiece, then attach tailpiece by screwing a slip nut onto sink strainer (photo above). If necessary, tailpiece can be cut to fit with a hacksaw.

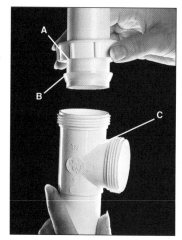

Slip nut (A), *slip washer (B), waste-T (C).*

3 On sinks with two basins, use a continuous waste T-fitting to join the tailpieces (photo bottom left). Attach the fitting with slip washers and nuts. Bevelled side of washers faces threaded portion of pipes.

4 Attach the trap arm to the drain stub-out, using a slip nut and washer. Bevelled side of washer should face threaded drain stub-out. If necessary, trap arm can be cut to fit with a hacksaw.

5 Attach trap bend to trap arm, using slip nuts and washers. Bevelled side of washers should face trap bend. Tighten all nuts with groove joint pliers.

Installing a Dishwasher

A dishwasher requires a hot water supply connection, a drain connection and an electrical hookup. These connections are easiest to make when the dishwasher is located next to the sink.

Hot water reaches the dishwasher through a supply tube. With a multiple-outlet shutoff valve or brass T-fitting on the hot water pipe, you can control water to the sink and dishwasher with the same valve.

For safety, loop the dishwasher drain hose up through an air gap mounted on the sink or countertop. An air gap prevents a clogged drain from backing up into the dishwasher. Follow manufacturer's directions for installation method.

A dishwasher requires its own 20-amp electrical circuit.

TIP:

The dishwasher drain hose is looped up through an air gap device attached to the sink or countertop. An air gap is a safety feature that prevents dirty water from backing up into the dishwasher.

How to Install a Dishwasher

1 Mount air gap, using one of the pre-drilled sink openings. Or, bore a hole in the countertop with a drill and hole saw. Attach the air gap by tightening mounting nut over the tailpiece with groove joint pliers.

2 Cut openings in side of sink base cabinet for electrical and plumbing lines, using a drill and hole saw. Dishwasher instructions specify size and location of openings. Slide dishwasher into place, feeding rubber drain hose through hole in cabinet. Level the dishwasher.

3 Attach the dishwasher drain hose to the special waste-T sink tailpiece nipple with a hose clamp.

4 Connect dishwasher supply tube to hot water shutoff, using groove joint pliers. This connection is easiest with a multiple-outlet shutoff valve or a brass T-fitting.

5 Remove access panel on front of dishwasher. Connect a brass L-fitting to the threaded opening on the dishwasher water valve, and tighten with groove joint pliers.

6 Run the braided steel supply tube from the hot water pipe to the dishwasher water valve (photo below left). Attach supply tube to L-fitting, using groove joint pliers.

7 Remove cover on electrical box. Run power cord from outlet through to electrical box. Strip about a ½" of insulation from each cord wire, using combination tool. Connect black wires, using a wire-connector. Connect white wires. Connect green insulated wire to ground screw (photo bottom right). Replace box cover and dishwasher access panel.

Water valve (A), L-fitting (B).

Cover (A), box (B), ground screw (C).

MASTERCRAFT

BASIC HAND TOOLS

- adjustable wrench/Robo-Grip pliers
- ratchet

NEEDED MATERIALS

- wax ring & sleeve
- plumber's putty
- floor bolts
- tank bolts with rubber washers
- seat bolts and mounting nuts

NOTE: With some toilets, you will need to purchase a flush handle, fill valve and flush valve separately.

TIP:

Install a toilet by anchoring the bowl to the floor first, then mounting the tank onto the bowl. China fixtures crack easily, so use care when handling them.

Installing Toilets

Most toilets in the low-to-moderate price range are two-piece units, with a separate tank and bowl, made of vitreous china. One-piece toilets, with integral tank and bowl, also are available, but the cost is usually two or three times that of two-piece units.

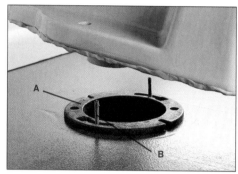

Toilet flange (A), *floor bolt (B).*

How to Install a Toilet

1 Turn bowl upside down and place a new wax ring and sleeve onto the toilet outlet. Apply a ring of plumber's putty around the bottom edge of the toilet base.

2 Position the toilet over the toilet flange so the floor bolts fit through the holes in the base of the toilet (photo above). The flange should be clean, and the floor bolts should point straight up.

3 Press down on the toilet bowl to compress the wax ring and plumber's putty. Attach washers and nuts to the floor bolts, and tighten with an adjustable wrench until snug. Do not overtighten. Attach trim caps.

4 Turn the tank upside down, and set the spud washer over the tailpiece of the flush valve. Turn tank right side up.

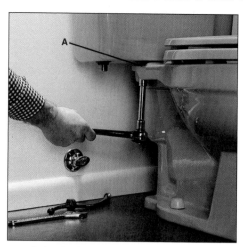

Tank bolt (A).

5 Set the tank onto the bowl, centring the spud washer over the water inlet opening near the back edge of the bowl.

6 Shift the tank gently until the tank bolt holes in the tank are aligned over the tank bolt holes in the bowl flange. Place rubber washers onto tank bolts, then insert the bolts down through the holes in the tank.

7 From beneath the bowl flange, attach washers and nuts to the tank bolts, and tighten with a ratchet wrench or basin wrench until snug (photo above). Do not overtighten.

8 Cut a piece of supply tube to fit between the shutoff valve and the toilet tank. Attach the tube to the shutoff valve, then to the fill valve tailpiece. Use an adjustable wrench to tighten coupling nuts until they are snug.

9 Mount the toilet seat onto the bowl by tightening the mounting nuts onto the seat bolts from below the seat flange.

Installing Showers

Use pre-fabricated shower panels and a plastic shower base to build an inexpensive, easy-to-install shower stall. Building Codes require that each home have a tub in at least one bathroom, but in spare bathrooms or guest bath, you can replace the tub with a shower stall to create space for storage or a second sink. Ceramic tile for custom showers is installed the same way as ceramic wall tile (pages 26-27).

How to Frame a Shower Alcove

1 Measure shower base, and mark dimensions on floor. Measure from centre of drain pipe to ensure the drain will be centred in the shower alcove, install blocking between studs in existing walls to provide a surface for anchoring alcove walls.

2 Build 2x4 alcove walls just outside the marked lines on the floor. Anchor the alcove walls to the existing wall and the subfloor. If necessary, drill holes or cut notches in the sole plate for plumbing pipes.

3 In the stud cavity that will hold the shower faucet and shower head, mark reference points 48" and 72" above the floor to indicate location of faucet and shower head.

4 Attach 1x4 cross braces between studs to provide surfaces for attaching the shower head and faucet. Centre the cross braces on the marked reference points, and position them flush with the back edge of the studs to pro-vide adequate space for the faucet body and shower head fittings.

5 Following manufacturer's directions, assemble plumbing pipes and attach faucet body and shower head fitting to cross braces. Attach the faucet handle and shower head after the shower panels have been installed.

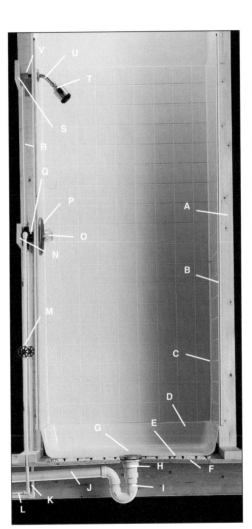

Anatomy of a shower: *shower framing members (A), water-resistant wallboard (B), tileboard shower surround (C), shower base (D), mortar base (E), subfloor (F), drain cover (G), drain tailpiece (H), drain P-trap (I), branch drain (J), cold supply pipe (K), hot supply pipe (L), shutoff valves (M), cross brace for faucet, 48" (N), faucet handle (O), escutcheon (P), faucet body (Q), shower pipe (R), cross brace for shower head, 72" (S), shower head (T), shower arm (U), elbow (V).*

RECOMMENDED POWER TOOLS

MASTERCRAFT

DRILL

RECOMMENDED HAND TOOLS

- basic hand tools
- level
- groove joint pliers
- hacksaw
- hole saw
- caulk gun
- Robo-Grip pliers

NEEDED MATERIALS

- 2x4, 1x4 lumber
- 10d nails
- pipe straps
- shower pipes & fittings
- dry-set mortar
- liquid soap
- wood screws
- wallboard screws
- panel adhesive
- carpet scrap
- tub & tile caulk

How to Install a Shower Base

1 Trim the drain pipe in the floor to the height recommended by the manufacturer, usually near or slightly above floor level (photo below). Stuff a rag into the drain pipe, and leave it in until you are ready to make the drain connections.

2 Prepare the shower drain piece as directed by the manufacturer, and attach it to the drain opening in the shower base. Tighten locknut securely onto drain tailpiece to ensure a waterproof fit.

3 Mix batch of dry-set mortar, then apply a 1" layer to subfloor, covering shower base area. Mortar stabilizes and levels the shower base.

4 Apply liquid soap to the outside of the drain pipe in the floor and to the inside of the rubber gasket in the drain tailpiece. Set the shower base onto the drain pipe, and press down slowly until the rubber gasket in the drain tailpiece fits snugly over the drain pipe.

5 Press the shower base down into the dry-set mortar, carefully adjusting it so it is level. If directed by manufacturer, anchor the shower base with screws driven through the edge flanges and into the wall studs. Let mortar dry for six to eight hours.

RECOMMENDED HAND TOOLS

- basic hand tools
- groove joint pliers
- hacksaw
- carpenter's level
- caulk gun
- Robo-Grip pliers/ adjustable wrench

NEEDED MATERIALS

- tub protector
- shims
- galvanized deck screws
- drain-waste-overflow kit
- liquid soap

- 1x3, 1x4 and 2x4 lumber
- galvanized roofing nails
- galvanized roof flashing
- tub & tile caulk

Installing Bathtubs

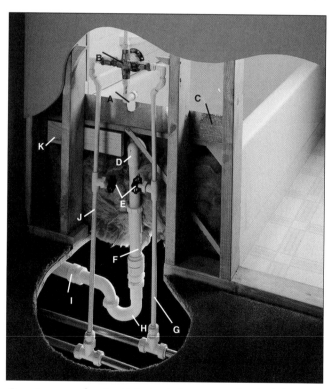

Anatomy of a bathtub: tub spout nipple (A), faucet body (B), flashing (C), overflow pipe (D), shutoff valves (E), drain tailpiece (F), hot water supply (G), P-trap (H), branch drain (I), cold water supply (J), tub ledger (K).

How to Install a Bathtub in an Alcove

1 Attach the faucet body and shower head to the water supply pipes, and attach the assembly to 1x4 cross braces before installing the tub. Trim the drain pipe to height specified by the drain-waste-overflow kit manufacturer.

2 Place a tub-bottom protector, which can be cut from the shipping carton, into tub. Test-fit the tub by sliding it into the alcove so it rests on the subfloor, flush against the wall studs.

3 Check tub rim with a carpenter's level, and shim below the tub to make it level. Mark the top of the nailing flange at each stud. Remove the bathtub from the alcove.

4 Measure the distance from the top of the nailing flange to the underside of the tub rim, and subtract that amount (usually about 1") from the marks on the wall studs. Draw a line at that point on each wall stud.

5 Cut ledger board strips, and attach them to the wall studs just below the mark for the underside of the tub rim (step 4). You may have to install the boards in sections to make room for any structural braces at the ends of the tub.

6 Adjust the drain-waste-overflow assembly (usually sold as a separate kit) to fit the drain and overflow openings. Attach gaskets and washers as directed by the manufacturer, then position the assembly against the tub drain and overflow openings.

7 Apply ring of plumber's putty to bottom of drain piece flange, then insert drain piece through the drain hole in the bathtub. Screw drain piece into drain tailpiece, and tighten until snug. Insert pop-up drain plug.

8 Insert drain plug linkage into the overflow opening, and attach the overflow coverplate with long screws driven into the mounting flange on the overflow pipe. Adjust drain plug linkage as directed by manufacturer.

9 Apply a ½"-thick layer of dry-set mortar to subfloor, covering entire area where tub will rest.

10 Lay soaped 1x4 runners across the alcove so they rest on the far sill plate. The runners will allow you to slide the tub into the alcove without disturbing the mortar base.

11 Slide the tub over the runners and into position, then remove the runners, allowing the tub to settle into the mortar (photo below). Press down evenly on the tub rims until they touch ledger boards.

12 Before the mortar sets, nail the tub rim flanges to the wall studs. Rim flanges are attached either by pre-drilling holes into the flanges and nailing with galvanized roofing nails, or by driving roofing nails into studs, so the head of the nail covers the rim flange. After rim flanges are secured, allow mortar to dry six to eight hours.

13 Attach 4"-wide strips of galvanized metal roof flashing over tub flange to help keep water out of the wall. Leave a ¼" expansion gap between the flashing and the tub rim. Nail the flashing to each wall stud, using 1" galvanized roofing nails.

14 Adjust the drain tailpiece so it will fit into the P-trap (you may have to trim it with a hacksaw), then connect it, using a slip nut. Install wall surfaces, then install faucet handles and tub spout. Finally, caulk all around the bathtub.

- neon circuit tester
- wire stripper
- cable ripper
- level

NEEDED MATERIALS

- NM cable
- wire staples
- wire-connectors
- screws

Installing Electrical Bath Fixtures

Installing most bathroom lights is similar to installing lights in any other room in the house. Adding new lighting fixtures makes a bathroom safer and more inviting and can even make bathrooms seem larger. In showers, install only vapour-proof lights that have been approved for wet areas. Shower lights have a water-proof gasket that fits between the fixture and the light cover.

Running cables for new electrical fixtures is easiest if wall surfaces have been removed. Make the final wiring hookups at the fixtures after wall surfaces are finished.

Follow Local Code requirements for wiring bathrooms (see pages 10-11). Reduce shock hazard by protecting the entire bathroom circuit with GFCI receptacles.

If you are not confident in your skills, have an electrician install and connect fixtures. Unless you are very experienced, leave the job of making circuit connections at the main service panel to an electrician.

CAUTION: Always shut off electrical power at the main service panel, and test for power before working with wires.

TIP:
Be extra careful when working with wiring in a bathroom around water. Always turn off electrical power at the main service panel before you begin an electrical project.

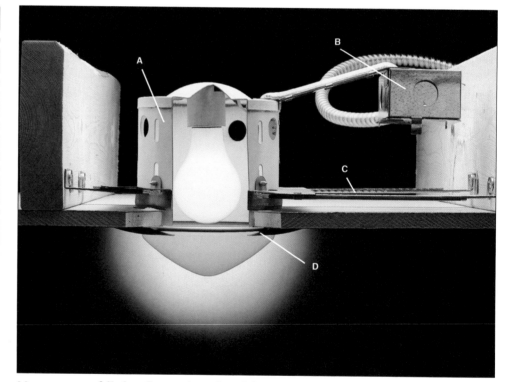

Vapourproof light: *fixture housing (A), wire connection box (B), mounting bracket (C), waterproof gasket (D).*

Install a GFCI receptacle and switch by making the following connections: black wire from power source (A) to brass screw marked LINE on GFCI; white wire from power source (B) to silver screw marked LINE; white wire to light (C) to silver GFCI screw marked LOAD; black wire to light (D) to a screw terminal on switch. Cut a short length of black wire (E), and attach one end to brass GFCI screw marked LOAD, and other end to a screw terminal on switch. Connect a bare grounding pigtail wire to GFCI grounding screw (F), and join all bare grounding wires (G) with a wire-connector. Tuck wires into box, then attach switch, receptacle and coverplate.

How to Install a Bathroom Light Fixture

1 Turn power off. Remove coverplate from light fixture, and feed the electrical cable through the hole in the back of the fixture (photo below). **NOTE:** Some bathroom lights have a connection box that is separate from the light fixture.

2 Position the fixture in the planned location, and adjust it so it is level. (Centre the fixture if it is being installed over a medicine cabinet or mirror.) If possible, attach the box at wall stud locations. If studs are not conveniently located, anchor the box to the wall, using

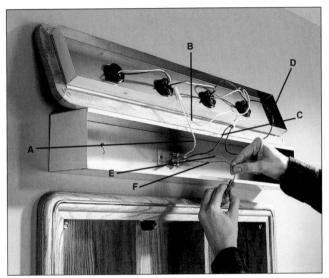

toggle bolts or other connectors.

3 Make electrical connections (photo above): attach white wire from cable (A) to white fixture wire (B), using a wire-connector; attach black wire from cable (C) to black fixture wire (D); connect bare copper grounding wire from cable (E) to the fixture grounding wire (F) (or attach to grounding screw in some fixtures).

4 Tuck the wires into the back of the box, then attach the fixture coverplate. Install unprotected light bulbs only after the rest of the remodelling project is completed.

Cable clamp (A).

MASTERCRAFT

JIGSAW

MASTERCRAFT

DRILL

MASTERCRAFT

RECIPROCATING SAW

RECOMMENDED HAND TOOLS

- basic hand tools
- caulk gun
- wire stripper
- screwdriver bits

NEEDED MATERIALS

- wallboard screws
- 2" dimension lumber
- NM cable (14-2, 14-3)
- wire-connectors
- electrical box
- hose clamps
- pipe insulation
- switches
- roofing cement
- self-sealing roofing nails

Installing a Vent Fan

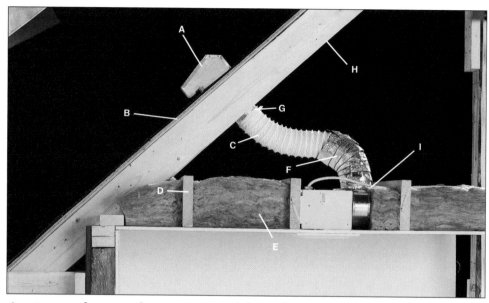

Anatomy of a vent fan: *vent cover (A), roof sheathing (B), vent hose (C), ceiling joist (D), insulation (E), pipe insulation (F), vent tailpiece (G), rafter (H), NM cable from power source (I).*

Building Codes usually require that all bathrooms without natural ventilation be equipped with a vent fan, but even if your bathroom has a window, installing a vent fan is a good idea.

Vent fans with only a light fixture usually may be wired into your main bathroom electrical circuit, but units with built-in heat lamps or blowers require a separate electrical circuit. Do not install a vent fan unit in the tub or shower area unless it is GFCI-protected and rated for use in wet areas.

Check the information label and choose a vent fan unit with a fan rating at least 5 CFM (cubic feet per minute) higher than the square footage of your bathroom. The SONE rating refers to the relative quietness of the unit, rated on a scale of 1 (quietest) to 7.

How to Install a Vent Fan

1 Position vent fan unit against a ceiling joist. Outline vent fan onto the ceiling, from above. Remove unit, then drill pilot holes at corners of the outline and cut out with a jigsaw or wallboard saw.

2 Remove grille from fan box, then position box against a joist, with the edge recessed 1/4" from finished surface of the ceiling (so the grille can be flush-mounted). Attach box to joist, using wallboard screws.

3 Mark and cut opening for switch box on wall next to the latch side of the bathroom door, then run a 14-gauge, 3-wire NM cable from switch cutout to vent fan unit.

4 Strip 10" of sheathing from end of the cable, then feed cable into switch box so at least 1/2" of sheathing extends into box. Tighten mounting screws until box is secure.

5 Strip 10" of sheathing from the end of the cable at the vent box, then attach the cable to a cable clamp. Insert the cable into the fan box. From inside of box, screw a locknut onto the threaded end of the clamp.

6 Mark the exit location in the roof for vent hose, next to a rafter. Drill a pilot hole, then saw through the sheathing and roofing material with a reciprocating saw to make the cut-out for the vent tailpiece.

7 From outside, remove section of shingles from around the cut-out, leaving roofing paper intact. Exposed area should be the size of the vent cover flange.

8 Attach a hose clamp to the rafter next to the roof cut-out, about 1" below the roof sheathing. Insert the vent tailpiece into the cut-out and through the hose clamp, then tighten the clamp screw.

9 Slide one end of vent hose over the tailpiece, and slide the other end over the outlet on the fan unit. Slip hose clamps or straps around ends of vent and tighten.

10 Wrap vent hose with pipe insulation. Insulation prevents moist air inside hose from condensing and dripping down into fan motor.

11 Apply roofing cement to bottom of vent cover flange, then slide vent cover over tailpiece. Nail the vent cover flange in place with self-sealing roofing nails, then patch in shingles around cover.

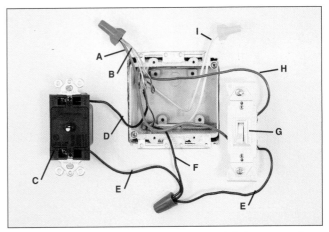

Wall switch box: grounding pigtail (A), grounding wires (B), timer (C), circuit wire from vent fan (D), pigtail wire (E), circuit wire from power source (F), single-pole switch (G), circuit wire from vent fan (H), neutral wires (I).

12 With the power shut off, make the following wire connections at the fan box (photo below): black circuit wire from timer to wire lead for fan motor; red circuit wire from single-pole switch to wire lead for light fixtures; white neutral circuit wire to neutral wire lead; circuit grounding wire to grounding lead in fan box. Attach coverplate over box when wiring is completed.

13 Connect fan motor plug to built-in receptacle on wire connection box, and attach fan grille to frame, using mounting clips included with the fan kit.

14 At wall switch box, add black pigtail wires to one screw terminal on the timer and to one screw terminal on the single-pole; add a green grounding pigtail to grounding screw on single-pole switch. Make the following wire connections: black circuit wire from power source to black pigtail wires; black circuit wire from vent fan to remaining screw on timer; red circuit wire from vent fan to remaining screw on single-pole switch. Join white wires with a wire-connector. Join grounding wires with a green wire-connector.

15 Tuck wires into wall switch box, then attach switches to box and attach coverplates and timer dial. Turn on power.

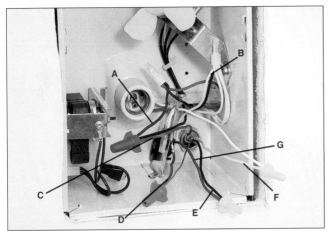

Wire lead to light fixtures (A), neutral wires (B), circuit wire from wall switch (C), grounding lead (D), circuit wire from timer (E), neutral circuit wire (F), wire lead to fan motor (G).

Index